High-Perform
FORD
FOCUS
Builder's Handbook

RICHARD HOLDENER

CarTech®
Auto Books & Manuals

Edited By: Steve Hendrickson

ISBN 1-884089-89-5

Order No. SA90

Printed in China

CarTech®, Inc.,
39966 Grand Avenue
North Branch, MN 55056
Telephone (651) 277-1200 • (800) 551-4754 • Fax: (651) 277-1203
www.cartechbooks.com

OVERSEAS DISTRIBUTION BY:

Brooklands Books Ltd.
P.O. Box 146, Cobham, Surrey, KT11 1LG, England
Telephone 01932 865051 • Fax 01932 868803
www.brooklands-books.com

Brooklands Books Aus.
3/37-39 Green Street, Banksmeadow, NSW 2109, Australia
Telephone 2 9695 7055 • Fax 2 9695 7355

Front Cover: *With just 5 psi of boost, this Jackson Racing Supercharged SVT Focus produced over 200 horsepower at the wheels.* (photo by Richard Holdener and Lisa Estrada)

Front Cover, Inset: *Here is the combination that the SVT Focus should have come with from the factory.*

Back Cover, Right: *The F-Max turbo motor eventually produced 300 wheel horsepower on a modified Zetec motor.*

Back Cover, Left: *Supercharged motors respond well to free-flowing air intake systems*

Back Cover, Lower: *With a carbon fiber hood, 18-inch wheels, and Baer racing brakes, you better be packing some serious horsepower. This SVT had over 200 wheel horsepower courtesy of a Jackson Racing supercharger.*

TABLE OF CONTENTS

About the Author 5

Introduction 6

Chapter 1 **Better Breathing — Air Intake Systems, Filters and Mass Air Meters** 8
Test 1 Stock versus Borla Drop-In Filter (Stock Zetec) 10
Test 2 Stock versus AEM Air Intake (Mild Zetec) 10
Test 3 Stock versus RS Akimoto Air Intake (Mild Zetec) 12
Test 4 Long versus Short Air Intake (Mild Zetec) 13
Test 5 Stock versus ProM MAF (19 lb Calibration) 13
Test 6 ProM 30 versus ProM 36 calibration (Supercharged Zetec) 15
Test 7 Large versus Small Air Filter (Turbocharged Zetec) 17
Test 8 Stock versus Jackson Racing Intake Upgrade (Supercharged Zetec) ... 18
Test 9 Stock versus Jackson Racing Intake Upgrade (Supercharged SVT) ... 18

Chapter 2 **Tuned for Torque — Throttle Bodies & Intake Manifolds** 21
Test 1 Stock versus 65mm Throttle Body (Mild Zetec) 23
Test 2 Stock versus 65mm Throttle Body (Supercharged Zetec) 24
Test 3 Stock versus 65mm Throttle Body (Turbocharged Zetec) 25
Test 4 Long versus Killer Bee Adjustable Intake (Mild Zetec) 26
Test 5 Intake Shoot-Out (Turbocharged Zetec) 29
Test 6 Long versus Short Runners on SVT Intake (Wild NA Zetec) 31
Test 7 Effect Of Runner Length (Supercharged & NA Zetec) 32
Test 8 Ford Racing versus Focus Central Composite Intakes (Wild Turbo Zetec) ... 35

Chapter 3 **Deep Breathing Exercises — Heads, Cams & Sprockets** 36
Test 1 Stock versus AEM Adj Cam Sprockets (Stock Zetec) 37
Test 2 Stock versus Focus Central Adj Cam Sprockets (Supercharged Zetec) ... 39
Test 3 Stock versus Focus Central Adj Cam Sprockets (Modified NA Zetec) ... 40
Test 4 Stock versus AEM Adj Cam Sprockets (Turbocharged Zetec) 42
Test 5 Stock versus Focus Central Head Package (Modified Zetec) 42
Test 6 Stock versus Focus Central Head Package (Supercharged Zetec) ... 44
Test 7 Stock versus Focus Central Adj Cam Sprockets (Stock SVT) 46

Chapter 4 **We Have Ignition — Chips, Ignitions, Plugs, & Pulleys** 48
Test 1 Stock versus Diablo Chip (Mild Zetec) 49
Test 2 Effect of Ignition Timing (Supercharged Zetec) 49
Test 3 Effect of Ignition Timing (Turbocharged Zetec) 52
Test 4 Stock versus Under Drive Pulley (Mild Zetec) 52
Test 5 Stock versus Nitrous (Mild Zetec) 55
Test 6 Pectel Engine Management Tuning (Wild Turbo Zetec) 56
Test 7 Redline Synthetic Oil (NA Zetec) 56
Test 8 Effect of Ignition Timing (Wild Turbo Zetec) 58

Chapter 5   **Exhaust Flow to Go — Headers & Cat-Back** **60**

Test 1   Stock versus Borla Cat-Back Exhaust (Mild Zetec) 61
Test 2   Stock versus JBA Shorty Header (Mild Zetec) 62
Test 3   JBA versus Long Tube Headers & No Cat (Modified Zetec) 64
Test 4   Stock cat versus Off-Road Pipe (Turbo Zetec) 64
Test 5   4:1 Long Tube versus Tri-Y Long Tube (Modified Zetec) 66
Test 6   Stock versus Off-Road Pipe versus Focus Central Long Tube Header (Mild SVT) 68
Test 7   Borla Cat-Back versus No Exhaust (Turbo Zetec) 69
Test 8   Stock cat versus Off-Road Pipe (NA Zetec) 71

Chapter 6   **Boost Builders — The Science of Supercharging** **73**

Test 1   Stock versus Jackson Racing M45 Supercharger (Stock Zetec) 74
Test 2   Stock versus Jackson Racing Big-Boost Upgrade (Supercharged Zetec) . . . 74
Test 3   Stock versus JR M62 Prototype Blower (Modified NA Zetec) 77
Test 4   Stock versus Jackson Racing Blower (SVT) 78
Test 5   Effect of Boost Reference Line (Supercharged Zetec) 81
Test 6   Effect of Boost Pressure Increase (Supercharged Zetec) 81

Chapter 7   **Under Pressure — The Technology of Turbocharging** **83**

Test 1   Stock versus Gude Turbo Kit (Stock Escape Zetec) 84
Test 2   Stock versus F-Max Turbo Kit (Mild Zetec) 84
Test 3   Effect of Increased Boost Pressure (Turbo Zetec) 87
Test 4   .48 A/R Ratio versus .63 A/R Ratio (Turbo Zetec) 87
Test 5   365-hp Innovative Turbo (Turbo Zetec) 90
Test 6   Effect of Boost Reference Line (Turbo Zetec) 91
Test 7   Duttweiller/Innovative Turbo Kit (Modified Turbo Zetec) 93
Test 8   Effect of Boost (Wild Turbo Zetec) 94
Test 9   Stock versus Pectel Turbo Kit (Mild Zetec) 94

Chapter 8   **Mild to Wild — Zetec Engine Buildups** **97**

Test 1   190-HP Focus Central Street Zetec Motor 97
Test 2   13-Second (237 hp) Supercharged Zetec Build Up 100
Test 3   300 Wheel Horsepower F-Max Turbo Build Up 102
Test 4   12-Second All-Motor Zetec Build Up 104
Test 5   514 Wheel Horsepower Turbo Zetec Build Up 107

Chapter 9   **Dropped & Stopped — Canyon Carvers and Better Binders** **110**

Hyland's Dynamic Suspension 110
Attitude Adjustment: Focus Central Coil-Over Suspension 114
Putting the "S" in SVT: Installing Coil-Over Suspension 117
Building Better Binders: ZX3 Rear Disc Brake Upgrade 120
Getting Hooked Up: Clutch, Flywheel, and Limited Slip Diff Install 121

Appendix A   **Ford Focus Performance Source Guide** **125**

ABOUT THE AUTHOR

If you're looking for Richard Holdener, try the closest chassis or engine dyno, as he spends the majority of his time testing performance components. "As far back as I can remember, I was fascinated with performance products — specifically how each component affected the power curve. And magazine articles usually produced more questions than answers. Before chassis dynos became commonplace, magazines relied on the old seat-of-the-pants to verify power claims made by manufacturers. Unfortunately, most of these derriere dynos were somewhat less than accurate. Once dynos became affordable, performance claims could be verified more accurately."

Holdener works as a technical editor for a number of magazines, and writes a monthly column in *Muscle Mustangs & Fast Fords* magazine on forced induction. Instead of covering everything from car shows to racing events, Holdener specializes in tech articles. A great deal of his dyno testing experience has come from Holdener's participation in road racing and land speed records. As an engine builder and driver, Holdener has set G/PRO and G/BALT land speed records at both Bonneville and El Mirage, as well as a national road race championship in the United States Touring Car Championship. "If I'm not on the dyno, I'm building a car or trying to find someone to let me drive."

Holdener's fascination with fast Fords began when he bought a 1988 Ford 5.0L Mustang LX, a car he still owns. "I originally purchased the Mustang to compete in SCCA Showroom Stock SSGT class against the Camaros. Unfortunately, shortly after I got the car ready for competition, Chevy offered the 1LE performance package, and the Mustang brakes simply were no match for the Camaro's. Ironically, about this time I started working on staff at *All Chevy* magazine. The staff gave me more than a few strange looks as I pulled up to write about everything Chevys driving a Mustang. But I'm not a Chevy or Ford man, I just like performance. No matter what I have, domestic or import, I want to improve that car's performance."

This desire for improved performance got the best of Holdener when Ford offered him a 2001 Focus ZX3. The ZX3 was an excellent car, offering exceptional handling and decent performance from the 2.0L Zetec motor. Naturally the SVT version was a significant step up from the standard model, but both models could offer much greater performance with the right modifications — but which modifications were "right?" After endless hours on the dyno and thousands of dyno runs, Holdener discovered just how much power was available from the 2.0L Zetec and SVT Focus motors. "The only real way to discover the effectiveness of any particular component or combination is to subject them to dyno testing. Speculation about things like header size, intake runner length and turbo boost levels can be meaningless without dyno testing." *High-Performance Ford Focus Builder's Handbook* is the result of this extensive dyno-testing program.

While it is impossible to test every possible aftermarket component on every possible combination, Holdener went to great lengths to illustrate the power gains available from a wide variety of different performance components. In this book, individual chapters are dedicated to specific performance components. Thus, intake manifolds, camshafts, and turbochargers all have their own chapter.

Sometimes testing reveals that there is actually the need for more testing. The dyno testing run on the throttle bodies is a perfect example. "After examining the stock Zetec throttle body, it seemed obvious that the design was not optimum for maximum airflow. While the visual examination indicated that stock throttle body was inadequate, dyno testing illustrated otherwise. Dyno testing the stock throttle body on a stock motor resulted in almost no power gain. Since the throttle body was simply an air valve, would a wilder combination benefit from the additional airflow offered by a larger throttle body?" Thus, accurately testing a simple 65mm throttle body required four different power levels and engine configurations.

Holdener also stresses that engine modifications are not all there is to building a high-performance car. Faster cars need faster stops and improved handling, so the final chapter covers a couple of suspension and brake upgrades for the Focus.

In addition to this book, Holdener has also written *5.0L Ford Dyno Tests*, *Building Short Track Ford Power*, and *How To Build Honda Horsepower* for S-A Design.

Dyno Testing

The Ford Focus was a success even before the aftermarket started coming out with air intakes, cams and turbochargers. Listed as the best selling car in the world (as of this writing), Ford finally designed and built a sport-compact car that could compete with the imports. The Focus was blessed with good looks, nimble handling and reasonable fuel mileage. If there was a complaint about the Focus, it was the 2.0L Zetec power plant. Though torquey, the Zetec lacked the frantic top-end charged offered by Honda's VTEC motors, thus a Zetec-powered Focus was easy prey for anything sporting a VTEC badge. Ford changed this situation somewhat with the introduction of the 170-hp SVT version, but the vast majority of Foci are of the more pedestrian 130-hp Zetec variety. What the Zetec motor needed was a serious infusion of performance. This infusion of power came from the aftermarket.

Early in the development of performance components (especially forced induction), the 2.0L Zetec somehow earned a reputation for being weak internally. The story goes, enthusiasts were breaking the motors due to inferior quality. Unknowledgeable individuals pointed to the powdered-metal connecting rods as the weak link in the motor. How many Zetec motors actually came apart is still a mystery, but the numbers were certainly smaller than the internet would have you believe. Like the unintended acceleration fiasco with the Audis, the culprit turned out to be operator error. Early attempts at turbocharging the Zetec motor resulted in problems related to tuning and not internal strength. The main obstacle was the returnless fuel system. In the old days, adding a turbo required only an FMU to raise the fuel pressure under boost, but Ford eliminated this method of fuel enrichment when it opted to go with the returnless fuel system. Forced induction with no additional fuel spells nothing but trouble, something early turbo pioneers quickly found out.

The issue of adding performance components to a Zetec (or SVT) motor is complicated. Both Ford Focus motors (Zetec and SVT) come equipped with mass air meters. Because the system monitors the mass, temperature, and density of the air flowing into the motor, upgrades can be made. The reason for this is that the mass air meter will recognize the additional airflow produced by the performance components (for instance: header, cams or intake) and provide the necessary additional fuel to go with the additional mass flow. If you install a cold air intake, such as the system we tested from AEM, the mass air meter will recognize the additional flow (and possible temperature change) and provide the necessary fuel to keep the air/fuel ratio

Ford's Zetec 4-cylinder is a decent performer in stock form, but it can produce a lot more power with the judicious application of aftermarket parts. The trick is knowing which parts work, and in what combinations.

in line. The same goes for installing Stage 1 Crane cams, ported cylinder heads or a cat-back exhaust system. You might now be wondering why the mass air meter won't simply recognize the added airflow of a turbo or supercharger, and that is an excellent question.

The problems associated with forced induction are many. Even though the mass air meter will recognize the additional airflow, the fuel and timing curves were designed for a normally aspirated motor, one with stringent emission controls at that. As such, the desired air/fuel ratio would be much too lean (13.2:1) for a forced induction application, not to mention having excessive timing that could easily cause massive detonation. Another mass air meter problem is exceeding the meter's flow potential, or more specifically, the electronics of the meter. The stock MAF was designed to operate in a given mass (or power) range. The meter provides a voltage signal ranging from 1-5 volts based on the mass flow. Obviously, Ford engineers had no reason to equip the mass air meter on a 130-hp Zetec motor with the ability to monitor double or triple that maximum power level. It is possible (and likely) that installing a supercharger or turbocharger will top out the electronics of the stock mass air meter, regardless of the lean condition the readings are providing.

The final problem with excessive power gains using forced induction (or wild naturally aspirated combos) is that the stock fuel injectors will not flow enough to support the new power levels. The author's 2.0L Zetec motor came equipped with 19-pound injectors. Though more than sufficient to feed the needs of the stock 130-hp motor, the injector size limits the power output to around 160 horsepower, unless you are able to successfully raise the fuel pressure in the system. This is a difficult task, since the pressure in the returnless fuel system is controlled by the computer. The computer monitors the fuel pressure using a pressure transducer located on the fuel rail. Based on the readings provided by the transducer, the computer will modulate the pulse-width (think of the pulsing injector) of the fuel pump

to control the fuel pressure. This type of control makes it difficult to install larger fuel pumps and impossible to install inline pumps. The factory systems have become much more sophisticated, so must the enthusiasts.

This book was designed to demonstrate the power gains available from a wide variety of different performance components. The book includes real-world, back-to-back dyno testing of various components along with dedicated performance buildups. Whether you are looking for a wild supercharged, turbocharged, nitrous, or just a simple cold air intake, you'll find results in these pages. The book includes dedicated chapters on air intake systems, intake

manifolds, throttle bodies, and cylinder head packages. Also covered are camshafts, cam sprockets, and custom chips. Want to know how well a Zetec motor runs with a dual-runner SVT intake? Its' in here. Just how much boost will a stock short block take? The chapter on turbocharging includes a 365-hp turbo motor running the stock Zetec short block (so much for the weak internal component theory). Both nitrous and supercharging are covered, as well as extensive testing on all types of exhaust systems. The book finishes off with some trick suspension and brake components. If you are looking for performance Focus answers, chances are you'll find them in these pages.

The only way to know for sure what works is to test those components on a dyno. Most of the tests in this book were performed on a DynoJet chassis dyno. If you don't have access to a dyno, you can use this information to plan your Focus' performance upgrades.

BETTER BREATHING

Air Intake Systems, Filters, and Mass Air Meters

For any internal combustion engine, processing air begins at the air intake system. That's why the first chapter in the book is dedicated to the components that make up the air inlet system. On the Focus (Base, Zetec and SVT), this system includes the air box, filter, mass air meter and associated tubing connecting all of the components. Like any OEM system, maximum performance was not the predominant design criteria behind the air inlet system. This is especially true of the housing securing the air filter. Rather than build an air intake system to produce maximum power, the Ford engineers were forced to take into account cost, intake noise production, and component longevity. Unfortunately for Focus enthusiasts, cost and noise considerations often counter absolute performance. We pay the price for all the wimps looking for nothing more than whisper-quiet transportation. Luckily, the aftermarket has plenty of answers to our performance questions.

While the factory Zetec air box is anything but optimum, don't expect major power gains simply by bolting on a cone filter and air tube of some sort. Even the trickest air intake system on the market won't produce huge power gains. Is it because the aftermarket doesn't know how to build a good air intake? Is it because the factory Ford inlet system is already optimized? Is it some conspiracy to keep the Zetec motors from performing like their VTEC namesakes? The answer is a resounding "No" on all counts. The reason installing a simple air intake system won't produce huge power gains is because the factory Zetec motor only requires 130-hp worth of airflow. The factory air intake system is just about capable of supplying that airflow to the stock motor. Even though an aftermarket air intake system may significantly out-flow the stock system, the motor doesn't need, and really can't benefit from, the additional airflow.

The air intake situation changes however, when you start making modifications to the motor to increase the power output. Check out the results of

It makes sense to start any performance project from the beginning. In the case of the Ford Focus motor, the beginning is the air inlet system.

test number 8 in Chapter One. Replacing the stock air intake system with a prototype system produced gains of 5 to 15 horsepower. Why such big power gains? The answer is that the test motor in question sported a Jackson Racing supercharger. Instead of producing 130 (motor) horsepower, the Zetec motor pumped out a good 40-50 hp more thanks the extra 5 psi of boost supplied by the blower. The additional airflow required by the supercharged motor taxed the airflow capacity of the stock inlet system. Improving the system with the installation of a prototype system fabricated by Jackson Racing reduced the airflow restrictions and increased the power output. If you compare the gains offered to the supercharged motor with those produced in normally aspirated trim, you will see a pattern emerge. The greater the airflow needs of the motor, the greater the power gains offered by a well-designed inlet system.

Test 1: Stock vs. Borla Drop-in Replacement Filter

Engine Specifications

Block:	Stock
Crank:	Stock
Rods:	Stock
Pistons:	Stock
Head:	Stock
Valves:	Stock
Cams:	Stock
Sprockets:	Stock
Intake:	Stock
Throttle body:	Stock
Air intake:	Stock
Filter(s):	Stock vs. Borla
Maf:	Stock
Header:	Stock
Exhaust:	Stock
Injectors:	Stock
Turbo:	NA
Blower:	NA
Boost level:	NA
Management:	Stock ECU
Fuel pump:	Stock
Intercooler:	NA
Nitrous:	No

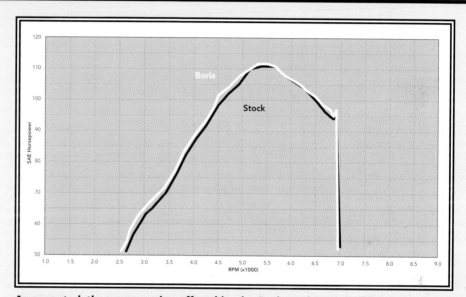

As expected, the power gains offered by the Borla replacement filter were minor. Oddly enough, the gains were most prevalent below the horsepower peak.

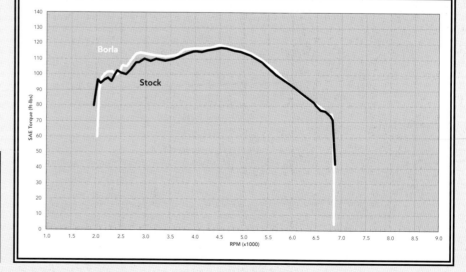

Replacing the stock filter was this closed-cell foam filter from Borla.

With the gains occurring low in the rev range, the torque improvements offered by the replacement filter were 3-4 ft-lbs.

Test 1
Stock versus Borla Drop-In Replacement Filter

Looking at the graph, the Borla filter was worth a few extra horsepower, though the power gains were never more than 2-3 horsepower. It should be evident by the results that installing a simple drop-in filter is worth very little in terms of added horsepower. This particular test was run on a 2001 ZX3 in stock trim. There were no modifications to the 2.0L Zetec motor other than replacing the stock paper-element filter with a performance filter from Borla

Test 1: The stock air box housed a rectangular paper-element air filter.

Performance. Though the Borla filter easily out-flowed the paper-element stock filter, the stock filter did not represent an airflow restriction at stock power levels. It should also be noted that the motor had less then 2000 miles on it and the stock filter was still clean and in near-new condition. As the miles accumulate, paper-element filters become clogged and the flow rate deteriorates. Serviceable filters such as those offered by Borla will not reduce performance as significantly as the paper-element filters, as their increased initial flow rate requires a great deal more contamination before the airflow is affected.

Test 2
Stock versus AEM Air Intake System

Immediately after running the Borla drop-in filter test, the 2001 Focus was subjected to another test. This time, the 2.0L Zetec motor was equipped with an AEM air intake system. Unlike many systems available for the Focus, the AEM system featured more than a length of tubing, a 90-degree bend and a

Test 2: It was necessary to remove the electronics from the factory mass air meter to install in the AEM intake system.

cone filter. AEM is one of the companies that understands the importance of not just airflow, but inlet air temperature. Installing a cone filter in the engine compartment can improve power compared to the stock air filter system, but the gains will not be as great as they can be, because the engine is breathing heated engine compartment air. Every effort should be made to allow the engine to breathe ambient air. AEM recognized this fact and designed an air intake system that positioned the free-flowing

Test 2: After installation, the AEM air intake/MAF system increased the power output of the Zetec motor by seven horsepower and 10 ft-lbs.

cone filter in the inner fenderwell. This position allowed the engine an unrestricted source of cool ambient air.

Another interesting feature of the AEM air intake system was the incorporation of the mass air meter as part of the air intake system. Unlike a simple cone filter system, the AEM intake replaced both the stock air box (& filter) and the stock mass air meter. This system elimi-

Test 1: The drop-in filter was the first test performed for this book. The 2.0L Zetec was completely stock, but the motor did not stay that way for long.

Test 2: Stock vs. AEM Air Intake System

Engine Specifications

Block:	Stock
Crank:	Stock
Rods:	Stock
Pistons:	Stock
Head:	Stock
Valves:	Stock
Cams:	Stock
Sprockets:	Stock
Intake:	Stock
Throttle body:	Stock
Air intake:	AEM (long)
Filter(s):	Cone
Maf:	AEM-part of the air intake system
Header:	Stock
Exhaust:	Stock
Injectors:	Stock
Turbo:	NA
Blower:	NA
Boost level:	NA
Management:	Stock ECU
Fuel pump:	Stock
Intercooler:	NA
Nitrous:	No

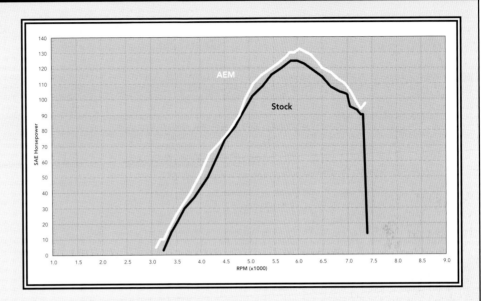

The gains offered by installation of the AEM air intake system were much more dramatic than the simple replacement filter.

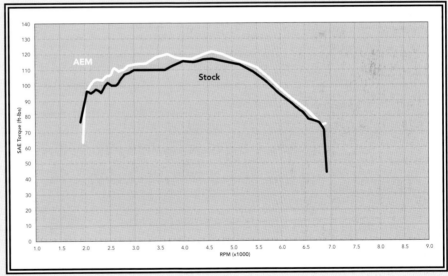

AEM offers this long air intake system to replace the factory air box.

The length of the AEM air intake system had a tuning effect on the power curve. Near 3,500 rpm, the AEM system improved the torque output by nearly 10 ft-lbs.

nated two potentially restrictive components in the intake system. Though the stock MAF was probably not much of a restriction on our stock motor, the AEM system would show even greater gains on a modified motor. Unlike the drop-in replacement filter, the AEM system was worth a significant gain in power. The AEM system added as much as 7 horsepower and 10 ft-lbs of torque at the wheels. Even more impressive was the fact that the AEM system improved the power output of the Zetec motor from idle to redline. While 7 horsepower and 10 ft-lbs of torque will not transform your Focus into a V8 beater, the power gains can be felt behind the wheel. With such a system, the motor is now ready to take on additional modifications like an exhaust system, header, and larger throttle body.

Test 3
Stock versus
Short Air Intake

This test was run on the 2.0L Zetec after installing a few other modifications. The spec sheet indicates that the motor was equipped with a JBA header (with stock cat), Borla cat-back exhaust, a 65mm throttle body and a Focus Central underdrive crank pulley. The results of each performance component can be seen in their respective chapters. The test was run to demonstrate the effectiveness of the more common shorty intake systems. In this instance, the air intake system consisted of removing the factory air box but retaining the plastic elbow connecting the throttle body to the mass air meter. By installing a cone filter over the stock mass air meter, we effectively built a short-style air intake system. The major difference between this intake test and the one run on the full-length AEM sys-

Test 3: Stock vs. Short Air Intake

Engine Specifications

Block:	Stock
Crank:	Stock
Rods:	Stock
Pistons:	Stock
Head:	Stock
Valves:	Stock
Cams:	Stock
Sprockets:	Stock
Intake:	Stock
Throttle body:	65mm Focus Central
Air intake:	Stock
Filter(s):	Stock vs. AEM
Maf:	Stock vs AEM
Header:	JBA
Exhaust:	Borla
Pulley:	Focus Central Underdrive
Injectors:	Stock
Turbo:	NA
Blower:	NA
Boost level:	NA
Management:	Stock ECU
Fuel pump:	Stock
Intercooler:	NA
Nitrous:	No

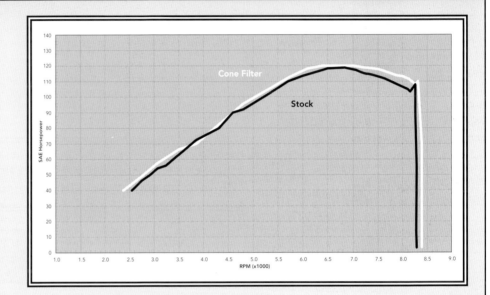

Adding the cone filter increased the peak power by just 2 horsepower, but the gains were as high as 5 hp elsewhere on the curve.

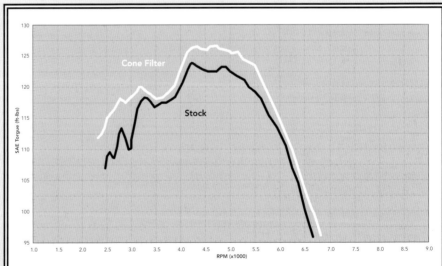

This test installed a cone filter over the stock mass air meter.

The cone filter offered significant torque gains down low.

Test 3: On the dyno, the cone filter improved power over the stock air box. The largest improvements offered by the cone filter were 6 horsepower and 8 ft-lbs, but remember that the tests were run with an open hood.

curve, the two intakes produced near-identical power. Check out 5400 rpm and 6300 rpm. Elsewhere, the shorty intake was the power champ. Unfortunately, this would not be the case on the street unless the cone filter was somehow surrounded by some sort of air box with ducting for ambient air. When running a comparable test on a VTEC Honda motor, the long and short length intakes produced similar results. Top-speed testing the Honda with each system revealed that the inlet air temperatures were much higher with the short air intake. The car was actually 2 mph faster with the long intake due to the change in air temperature. Something to think about!

Test 3: The stock Zetec air box was removed, but the MAF and length of tubing connecting the mass air meter to the throttle body were retained.

tem was the modifications to the motor. Note that the motor produced 118 wheel horsepower with the stock air intake. The exhaust, underdrive pulley, header and 65mm throttle body had noticeably increased the power output of Zetec motor. Replacing the stock air box with a cone filter increased the peak power output from 118 hp to 122 hp. The shorty system offered gains of 6 horsepower and 8 ft-lbs compared to the stock air intake system. Remember that these tests were run with an open hood and the gains on the street would be much less due to engine-compartment heat.

Test 4
AEM Long versus AEM Short Air Intake

The long and short air intakes make for an interesting comparison. Oddly enough, the length of the air intake has a tuning effect on the power curve generated by the motor. Note that the peak power numbers were within 1 horsepower, but that the curves fluctuated. From 2000 rpm to 3700 rpm, the long-style AEM intake out-powered the shorty intake. From 3700 rpm to red-line, the short intake held a slight power advantage. At some points along the

Test 5
Stock versus
Pro M Mass Air Meter-Stock
19-Pound Calibration

ProM supplied one of their mass air meters for this test. The mass air meter was calibrated for the stock 19-pound injectors, though ProM offers calibrations for a number of other larger injec-

Test 5: The stock mass air meter and air box assembly were only slightly restrictive to the near-stock Zetec motor.

Test 5: The ProM was calibrated for the stock 19-pound injectors. Credit the cone filter for most of the power gain offered at this power level.

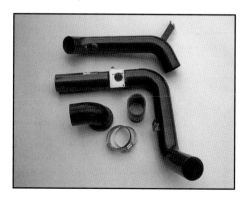

Test 4: The length of the air inlet system has a definite effect on the power curve. This long system from AEM really out-powered the short inlet system up to 3,600 rpm.

Test 4: AEM Long vs. AEM Short Air Intake

Engine Specifications

Block:	Stock
Crank:	Stock
Rods:	Stock
Pistons:	Stock
Head:	Stock
Valves:	Stock
Cams:	Stock
Sprockets:	Stock
Intake:	Stock
Throttle body:	65mm Focus Central
Air intake:	Stock vs. AEM shorty
Filter(s):	Stock vs. Borla
Maf:	Stock
Header:	JBA
Exhaust:	Borla
Pulley:	Focus Central Underdrive
Injectors:	Stock
Turbo:	NA
Blower:	NA
Boost level:	NA
Management:	Stock ECU
Fuel pump:	Stock
Intercooler:	NA
Nitrous:	No

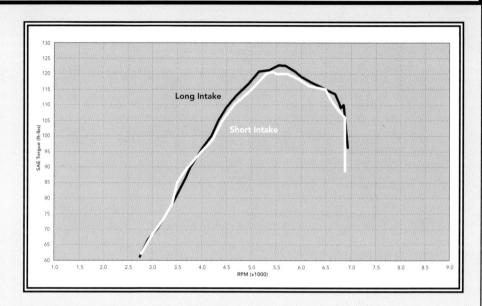

The long AEM system offered improved power production up to 3,700 rpm, then the shorter system took over up to redline.

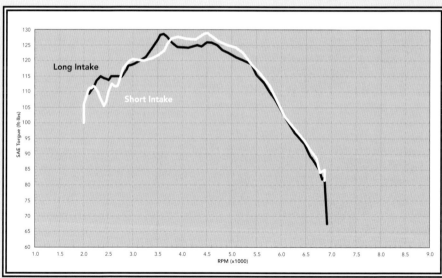

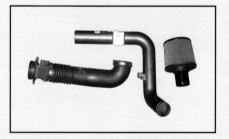

Check out the difference in length of the two inlet systems tested.

The long AEM system offered 6 ft-lbs. at 3,500 rpm, but torque suffered elsewhere compared to the short system.

tor combinations. The ProM meters were used successfully by the author on various supercharged and turbocharged Zetec motors at power outputs up to 270 wheel horsepower. In this test, the larger ProM meter was installed in place of the stock Ford mass air meter. The ProM improved the power output by as much as five horsepower. The reason for the rather limited power gain is the somewhat mild engine combination. The stock meter was simply not much of an airflow restriction to the mild Zetec motor. The larger ProM meter offered superior flow capability, but the motor was not able to take advantage of the additional flow. The ProM meter really shows its worth in subsequent tests with the Jackson Racing supercharger. On a stock or mild Zetec motor, the factory mass air meter works pretty well.

Test 5: Stock vs. ProM Mass Air Meter-Stock 19-Pound Calibration

Engine Specifications

Block:	Stock
Crank:	Stock
Rods:	Stock
Pistons:	Stock
Head:	Stock
Valves:	Stock
Cams:	Stock
Sprockets:	Stock
Intake:	Stock
Throttle body:	65mm Focus Central
Air intake:	Stock vs. Pro M
Filter(s):	Stock vs. Cone
Maf:	Stock vs Pro M
Header:	JBA
Exhaust:	Borla
Pulley:	Focus Central Underdrive
Injectors:	Stock
Turbo:	NA
Blower:	NA
Boost level:	NA
Management:	Stock ECU
Fuel pump:	Stock
Intercooler:	NA
Nitrous:	No

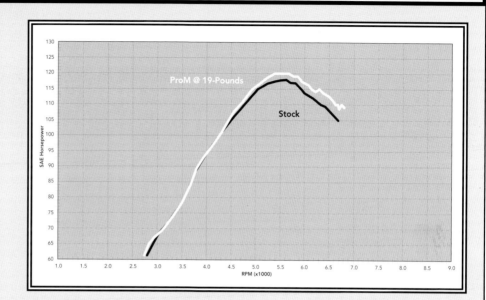

Installation of the ProM meter improved the power output 2 horsepower, but the gains were as high as 4-5 hp near the top.

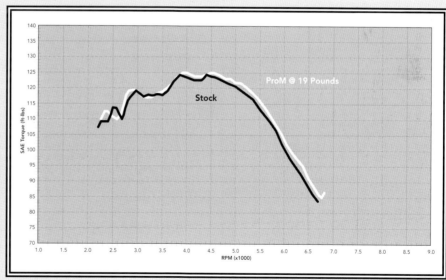

The ProM meter offered more airflow potential than the stock mass air.

The torque gains offered by the ProM meter were not present until 3,700 rpm.

Test 6
ProM Mass Air Meter/Injector Combo (30 lb. vs 36 lb.)

This test was run out of necessity, as we had exceeded the fuel-flow limit of the 30-pound injectors used with our Jackson Racing supercharged Zetec motor. Take a look at the graph illustrating the two air/fuel curves offered by the different meter/injector combinations. Running the Jackson Racing supercharger kit and the 30-pound injector/meter combination on the modified motor produced 212 horsepower. The problem was that the air/fuel curve indicated that the motor was leaning out once we reached 6200 rpm. The cure was to replace the 30-pound injectors with larger 36-pound injectors. Naturally the larger injectors were installed with a recalibrated ProM meter. Note that the power curves were nearly identical, but the air/fuel mixture remained safely below 12.0:1 all the way to 6800 rpm with the new meter/injector combination. The new combo allowed us to increase the blower speed to produce even more power, something not possible with the 30-pound injectors.

Test 6: To increase the fuel flow to the supercharged motor, we swapped out the 30-pound injectors and meter in favor of a set of larger 36-pound injectors and matching ProM meter. The increase in fuel flow allowed us to continue in our quest for additional horsepower.

Test 6: ProM Mass Air Meter/Injector Combo (30 lb. vs. 36 lb.)

Engine Specifications

Block:	Stock
Crank:	Stock
Rods:	Stock
Pistons:	Stock
Head:	Focus Central ported
Valves:	Stock
Cams:	Crane 210/206
Sprockets:	Focus Central adj
Intake:	JR Supercharged
Throttle body:	65mm Focus Central
Air intake:	Custom 3-inch aluminum tube
Filter(s):	Cone
Maf:	Pro M (30 cal vs. 36 cal)
Header:	Focus Central Long Tube
Flex Pipe:	Stock
Exhaust:	Borla
Pulley:	Stock
Injectors:	30 & 36
Turbo:	NA
Blower:	Jackson Racing M62
Boost level:	9 psi
Management:	Stock ECU
Fuel pump:	stock
Intercooler:	NA
Nitrous:	No

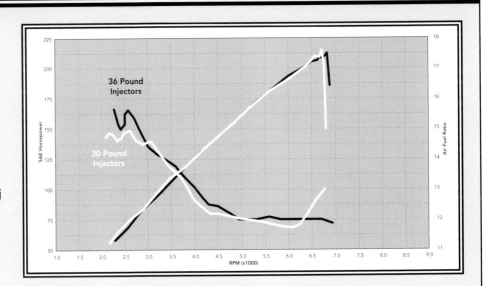

Note that the power curves were mirror images, but that the air/fuel curve began to get lean past 6,000 rpm with the smaller 30-pound injectors.

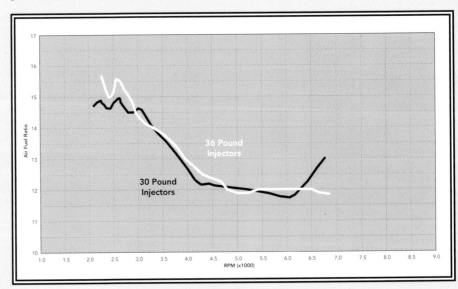

Isolating the air/fuel curve illustrates how the motor leaned out past 6,000 rpm. Near redline with the supercharged motor, the air/fuel mixture neared 13.0:1.

Test 6: Using the larger supercharger, we managed to surpass the flow capability of the 30-pound injectors.

Test 6: The tests were run on a Zetec motor equipped with a Jackson Racing supercharger. This particular prototype kit used on the author's Focus featured the larger M62 supercharger.

Test 7: We were concerned that the smaller cone filter was restricting our turbocharged motor. The dyno indicated that even the smaller of the two filters was more than adequate at our power level.

Test 7
Filter Test
Turbocharged Zetec

This test was run to satisfy the turbo owners out there who insist on running a turbocharger without an air filter. Made popular by the import drag racers, who insist on running their turbos with nothing more than a radiused air horn, street enthusiasts seem to think that a properly sized air filter restricts the power output. The reality is that air filters should be considered mandatory on turbo motors.

The last thing you want to do is have debris make its way to the impeller wheel. Turbos are very expensive, and since the right air filter can actually improve power, why take a chance?

This test involved running a pair of cone filters on the inlet system supplied

Test 7: Filter Test-Turbocharged Zetec

Engine Specifications

Block:	Stock
Crank:	Stock
Rods:	Stock
Pistons:	Stock
Head:	Focus Central Ported
Valves:	Stock
Cams:	Crane 210/206
Sprockets:	Focus Central Adjustable
Intake:	Stock
Throttle body:	65mm Focus Central
Air intake:	F-Max
Filter(s):	Small vs. large cone
Maf:	Pro M 36 cal
Header:	Focus Central Long Tube
Cat/off- road:	Focus Central·Off Road
Flex Pipe:	Stock
Exhaust:	Borla

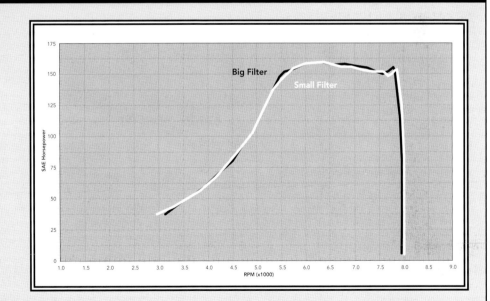

Testing filters on the turbo motor resulted in no change in power.

Pulley:	Stock	Management:	Stock ECU
Injectors:	36 lbs.	Fuel pump:	Stock
Turbo:	F-Max	Intercooler:	F-Max air-to-air
Blower:	NA	Ignition:	Crane
Boost level:	10 psi	Nitrous:	No

Test 7: Do turbo motors run best without an air filter? Don't believe what you read on the internet or see at import shootouts.

Test 7: A 300-hp turbo motor needs a big filter, right? Replacing the small cone filter with this sizable unit resulted in no gain in power.

by F-Max on their turbo kit. We suspected that the rather small air filter supplied with the kit might become a restriction at our elevated boost level of 10 psi. To find out, we swapped out the wimpy little filter and installed a replacement offering a significant increase in surface area. The results speak for themselves, as the turbo motor produced identical power with both filters. Apparently the little cone filter was more than sufficient for our boosted Zetec.

Test 8
Air Intake, MAF, & Filter
Jackson Racing
Supercharged Zetec

Installing the base (M45) Jackson Racing supercharger kit can add 45-50 additional horsepower to a normally aspirated Zetec motor. This test illustrated the benefits of replacing the stock air intake system and mass air meter with an upgrade offered by Jackson Racing. Adding the base 5 psi supercharger kit to an otherwise stock 2.0L Zetec motor will usually up the peak power to approximately 145 horsepower. This particular test motor was equipped with an aftermarket cat-

back exhaust system, so the peak power was up just a tad to just under 150 hp. The test involved replacing the stock mass air meter and air box with a prototype air intake system that incorporated the mass air electronics and a free-flowing cone filter. Obviously the factory inlet system was restricting the supercharged motor, as installing the prototype inlet system increased the power output from just under 150 horsepower to 164 hp. Though the peak torque only increased by 7 ft-lbs, the inlet system was responsible for a sizable increase across the rev range.

Test 9
Stock SVT Air Box vs.
Jackson Racing Air Intake
Supercharged SVT

Even more so than other forms of forced induction, positive displacement superchargers are very sensitive to inlet restrictions. The fact that they add so much extra airflow and power to the motor only compounds this problem. This sensitivity means that every effort must be made to minimize any type of restriction upstream of the blower. This includes the air filter, the mass air meter,

and the tube connecting the meter to the throttle body. Naturally, this also includes the throttle body itself, but the SVT is equipped with a sizable unit to begin with, so the restrictions generally occur before the throttle opening. Check out chapter two for information of the effects of installing a 65mm throttle body on combinations ranging from stock through wild all-motor to both forms of forced induction. You may be

Test 8: Adding a supercharger can dramatically improve the power output of a Focus motor, but it also places increased demands on the air inlet system.

Test 8: The prototype air inlet system required removal of the mass air electronics from the stock meter. The system also featured a free-flowing cone filter.

surprised how effective the stock (Zetec) throttle body was for certain applications. Hint – positive displacement supercharged motors like larger throttle bodies.

To illustrate the effectiveness of a revised inlet system on a supercharged SVT Focus, I ventured over to Jackson Racing to utilize both their DynoJet facility and their supercharged SVT Focus. Other than the installation of the prototype SVT supercharger kit (see chapter on supercharging), the SVT was bone stock. The Eaton M62 roots supercharger was set up to produce 4-5 psi and run with the stock SVT air box and filter assembly. In this condition, the supercharged SVT motor produced 181 hp. The numbers were slightly lower than I anticipated, but Oscar Jackson reminded me that the prototype was

---

Test 8: Air Intake, MAF, & Filter
Jackson Racing Supercharged Zetec

Engine Specifications

Block:	Stock
Crank:	Stock
Rods:	Stock
Pistons:	Stock
Head:	Stock
Valves:	Stock
Cams:	Stock
Sprockets:	Stock
Intake:	Stock
Throttle body:	65mm Focus Central
Air intake:	Stock vs. JR
Filter(s):	Stock vs. JR
Maf:	Stock vs. JR
Header:	Stock
Cat/off- road:	Stock Cat
Flex Pipe:	Stock
Exhaust:	Borla
Pulley:	Stock
Injectors:	Stock vs. 30 lbs.
Turbo:	NA
Blower:	ackson Racing
Boost level:	6 psi
Management:	Sock ECU
Fuel pump:	Stock
gnition:	Stock
Nitrous:	No

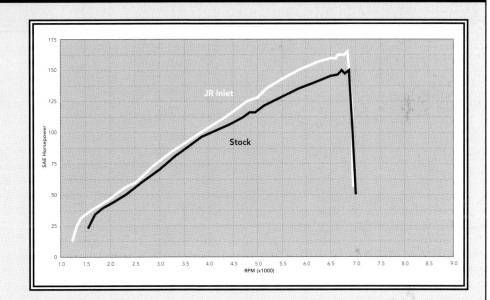

Superchargers, especially positive displacement superchargers, are very sensitive to inlet restrictions. Check out the power gains offered by replacing the factory air filter assembly with a revised system from Jackson Racing.

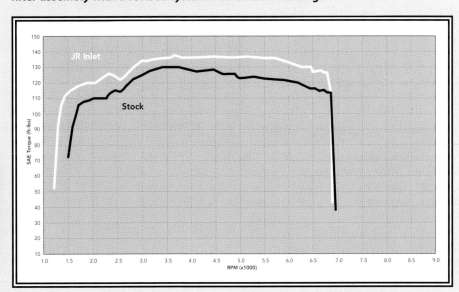

After installing the inlet tubing and cone filter, the supercharged motor picked up 14-15 horsepower.

The torque gains offered by the new inlet system were equally impressive.

---

down a full pound of boost to the production kits. After making back up runs to confirm the power numbers, I removed the stock air filter assembly and replaced it with a prototype air intake kit produced by Jackson Racing. The system included a 3-inch section of aluminum tubing to connect the mass air meter to the throttle body and a free-flowing cone filter. Running the super-charged SVT again with the new air inlet system resulted in a gain of 6-7 hp, the majority of which came past 5,200 rpm.

Test 9: Adding the prototype air intake system from Jackson Racing increased the power by 6-7 hp, with most of the gains coming near the top of the rev range.

Test 9: Stock SVT Air Box vs.
Jackson Racing Air Intake (Supercharged SVT)

Engine Specifications

Block:	Stock SVT
Crank:	Stock SVT
Rods:	Stock SVT
Pistons:	Stock SVT
Head:	Stock SVT
Valves:	Stock SVT
Cams:	Stock SVT
Sprockets:	Stock SVT
Intake:	Jackson Racing
Throttle body:	Stock SVT
Air intake:	Stock SVT vs JR
Filter:	Stock SVT vs JR
Maf:	Stock SVT
Header:	Stock SVT
Exhaust:	SVT
Injectors:	Stock SVT
Turbo:	NA
Blower:	Jackson Racing
Boost level:	5 psi
Management:	Stock ECU + JR Fuel Controller
Fuel pump:	Stock
Intercooler:	NA
Nitrous:	No

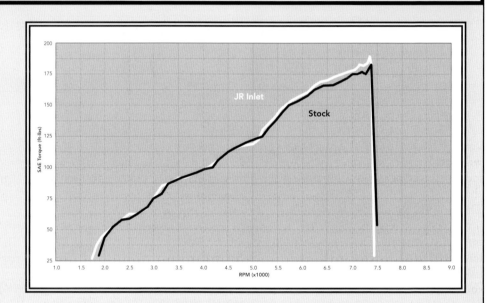

The SVT Focus was also responsive to a revised inlet system.

The Jackson Racing supercharged SVT Focus was run with the stock air filter assembly.

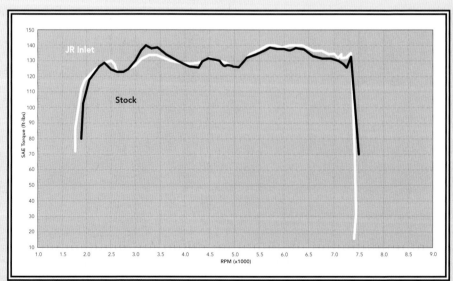

Most of the torque gains offered by the prototype inlet system came past 5,300 rpm.

TUNED FOR TORQUE

THROTTLE BODIES & INTAKE MANIFOLDS

Choosing the proper intake manifold is critical to the performance of your Zetec motor, as the intake design will determine not only where the motor makes peak power but also the shape of the remainder of the curve. Though a number of design criteria go into a performance intake manifold, the major determining factor is the runner length. Long runners help promote low-speed power production while short runners allow the motor to produce top-end horsepower. The composite intake used on the production 2.0L Zetec motor features intake runners measuring nearly 18 inches in length, some 6 inches longer than a typical VTEC Honda motor. Not surprisingly, the exceptionally long runners allow the Zetec motor to produce exceptional low-speed torque. In stock configuration, the 2.0L Zetec will produce a higher peak torque number than horsepower, something that can't be said of the VTEC import crowd. This low-speed torque production provides good throttle response and the illusion of a powerful motor. Unfortunately, the long runners don't allow the motor to breathe properly at higher engine speeds, and the stock Zetec peaks at 5300 rpm, falling off dramatically thereafter. With mild cam timing, small head ports and the long runners, the stock Zetec was definitely tuned for torque.

While the long intake runners limit high-rpm power production, short runners have their tradeoffs. You will see in this chapter that installing an intake manifold design that offers improved high-rpm breathing through shorter runners dramatically reduces the low-speed power production. Such is the tradeoff inherent in runner length. Naturally the intake design should be based on the intended usage and operating range. If you are building a dedicated race motor that has sufficient cam timing, compression, and head flow to allow an 8,000 rpm power peak (see 223-hp all motor buildup) and an operating range of 6,000 rpm to 8,200 rpm, then power production from 2,000-5,000 rpm would be unimportant. For a dedicated race motor, the idea is to maximize the average power production in the

More than any other component, the intake manifold is responsible for the shape of the power curve.

Test 1: Stock vs. 65mm Throttle Body (Mild NA Zetec)

Engine Specifications

Block:	Stock
Crank:	Stock
Rods:	Stock
Pistons:	Stock
Head:	Stock
Valves:	Stock
Cams:	Stock
Sprockets:	Stock
Intake:	Stock
Throttle body:	Stock vs 65mm
Air intake:	AEM
Filter:	AEM cone
Maf:	AEM
Header:	Stock
Exhaust:	Stock
Injectors:	Stock
Turbo:	NA
Blower:	NA
Boost level:	NA
Management:	Stock ECU
Fuel pump:	Stock
Intercooler:	NA
Nitrous:	No

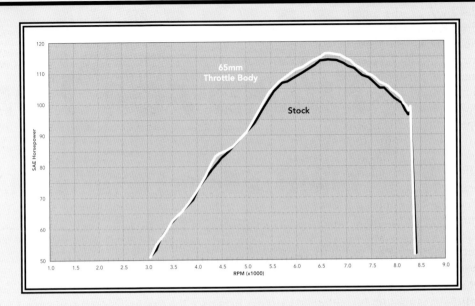

Though the internal orifice of the stock Zetec throttle body looks more than a tad restrictive, testing has shown that it flows well up to 200 wheel horsepower.

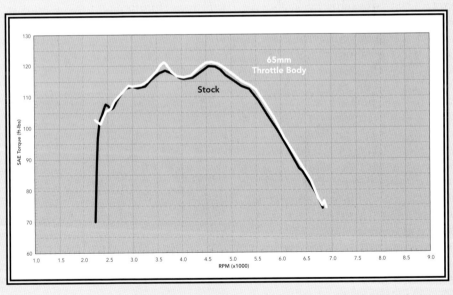

The gains offered by the larger 65mm throttle body were minimal on this mild Zetec motor.

The stock Zetec throttle was an odd design not conducive to optimum flow. The "ski jump" shape of the blade and reverse tapered bore produced an effectively rising rate throttle entry.

intended operating range. For this application, a short-runner intake would work best. Only testing could determine the most effective length for the application. At the time of this writing, Focus Central had done the most extensive intake manifold development for their race program.

While a race motor might well benefit from a short-runner intake, most street motors would not perform well with the same manifold. The reason is that the short runners will dramatically reduce the low-speed power production. Street motors spend the majority of their time at low engine speeds, revving from as low as 2000 rpm and accelerating up to 5500 rpm. In most cases, the shift rpm is even lower than 5500 rpm.

For a stock or mildly modified street motor, even one equipped with aftermarket cams and a ported cylinder head, the best choice would be an intake that offers longer runners. The ported stock intake offered by Focus Central, the adjustable intake (possibly in production by the time this reaches print) designed by the author, and even the Ford Racing intake (for wilder combinations) would be the best choices. Stay away from intakes offering less than 8 inches of runner length, as there will be a major penalty in power from 2,000 to 5,000 rpm, right where street motors spend most of their time.

What about turbo or blower motors? Does the runner length still affect power production with the presence of boost? The answer is *Absolutely Yes!* It is a common misconception that runner length has no affect on turbo and supercharged motors. The boost pressure has very little effect (at street boost levels) on the shape of the power curve of the motor. In testing, our normally aspirated Zetec motor produced peak power at 5,400 rpm without the turbo. Adding the F-Max turbo kit obviously elevated the power substantially, but the power peak only shifted by 100 rpm. You will note in this chapter that changing the intake manifold design (primarily runner length) had a dramatic effect on the shape of the power curve. Note that I use the phrase power curve as opposed to power output. In some cases, changes in intake design can produce an identical peak power number, but dramatically affect the rest of the curve. This is why it is important to show the entire curve rather than reference just the peak numbers. Peak power numbers are much less important than the average power production.

From a manufacturer's standpoint, the intake manifold runner length is at best a compromise. The runner length must be long enough to promote decent low-speed power production without limiting the RPM ability of the motor. Ford's Special Vehicle Team recognized the importance of intake runner length when building the SVT Focus. They equipped the SVT version with a dual-runner intake. Taking a cue from the B18C VTEC motor in the Acura Integra GSR, the SVT group attempted to optimize the power band by allowing the

motor to breathe through essentially two different intake manifolds. At low speeds, the intake uses long runners. At a predetermined engine speed, the long runner section is rotated out of the way to allow the motor to breathe through a shorter section, thus providing all the low-speed power of the long runners with the top-end power of the short runners. This dual-stage intake trickery is not new, as it has been employed by BMW, Mazda, and Toyota, in addition to Acura for their GSR.

One quick note on throttle bodies is in order. There seems to be some confusion on the effectiveness of larger throttle bodies. From a basic standpoint, a 65mm (or larger) throttle body will easily out-flow the stock Zetec throttle body. In the case of the 65mm throttle body offered by Focus Central, the difference in airflow is substantial. While the larger throttle body easily outflows the stock unit, installing a larger throttle body does not always equate to more power. Why does the improvement in airflow not improve power? The answer is that the larger throttle body only offers potentially more airflow. Power production is a function of air processed by the motor. If a restriction exists in that processing, additional power will be realized if you eliminate the restriction. In the case of the larger throttle body, the stock motor is not restricted by the stock throttle body. In fact, testing has shown that adding a 65mm throttle is not substantially beneficial until the power exceeds 175 wheel horsepower. Turbo motors are the exception, as the stock throttle body can be used effectively on motors exceeding 225 wheel horsepower thanks to the presence of boost pressure.

Test 1
Stock versus 65mm Throttle Body (Mild NA Zetec)

This was one of the earliest tests run on the author's personal 2001 ZX3. The motor was nearly stock, equipped with only an AEM cold air intake system. The AEM system was unique in that it included a dedicated mass air meter as part of the assembly. The intake tubing

Test 1: The Focus Central 65mm throttle body offered significantly more airflow (by 100+ cfm) over the stock throttle body. The real question is whether the stock throttle body represented a restriction to the stock motor.

included a section to remount the factory electronics removed from the stock mass air meter. In essence, the AEM air intake system included a mass air meter upgrade. Check out Chapter One (air intake systems) for more info on the AEM cold air system.

The remainder of the 130-hp Zetec motor was completely stock, right down to the catalytic converter and cat-back exhaust system. The stock motor produced 112 wheel horsepower and adding the AEM air intake system resulted in a gain of 2-3 peak horsepower. Adding the Focus Central 65mm throttle body resulted in a gain of 1-2 horsepower, with the majority of the gains coming after 4,000 rpm. Apparently the stock throttle body did not present much of a restriction at this power level. We do expect the gains offered by the larger throttle body to increase once we install it on a heavily modified or supercharged motor.

Test 1: Testing on the stock Zetec motor resulted in very little (if any) power gain. Apparently the stock Zetec throttle body supplied more than enough air to feed the stock combination.

Test 2
Stock versus 65mm Throttle Body (JR Supercharged Zetec)

At this writing, all-motor Zetec motors producing an honest 200 wheel horsepower are pretty few and far between. In my testing, I had run across a grand total of two motors approaching or eclipsing the magical 200-wheel horsepower mark, without the aid of nitrous or forced induction. While 200 all-motor wheel horsepower is a difficult task, producing 200 wheel horsepower with a supercharger is somewhat easier. I say somewhat here because even the supercharged version took some doing to finally break the 200 hp mark. Thanks to Jackson Racing, I was able to achieve my goal of not only topping 200 wheel horsepower (by a wide margin)

Test 2: Stock vs.
65mm Throttle Body (JR Supercharged Zetec)

Engine Specifications

Block:	Stock
Crank:	Stock
Rods:	Stock
Pistons:	Stock
Head:	Focus Central ported
Valves:	Stock
Cams:	Crane 210/206
Sprockets:	Focus Central
Intake:	Jackson Racing
Throttle body:	Stock vs. 65mm
Air intake:	Custom 3-inch
Filter:	Cone
Maf:	ProM
Header:	Focus Sport Long Tube
Exhaust:	Borla
Injectors:	36 lbs./hr.
Turbo:	NA
Blower:	Jackson Racing M62
Boost level:	12 psi
Management:	Stock ECU
Fuel pump:	Stock
Intercooler:	NA
Nitrous:	No

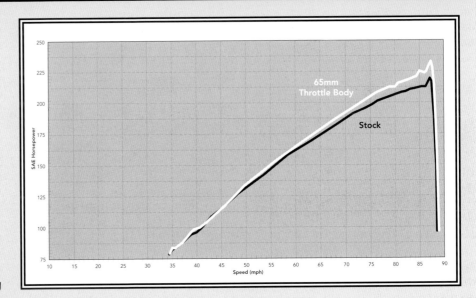

A larger throttle body is most beneficial when the power level has been increased, as was the case with our Jackson racing supercharged Zetec motor.

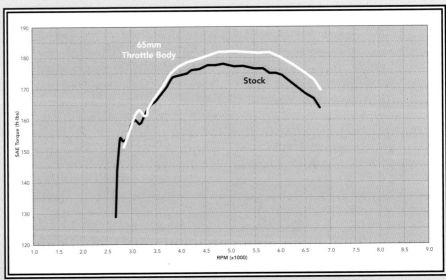

The supercharged Zetec motor responded well to the larger throttle body, to the tune of 12-13 horsepower.

The 65 mm throttle body offered a solid torque gain of 8-10 ft-lbs and as much as 12-13 horsepower.

Test 2: The Jackson Racing supercharger utilized a dedicated casting to adapt the 65mm throttle body to the inlet of the blower. The author port-matched the entry to the 65mm bore.

Test 2: This early Focus Central 65mm throttle body was run on the blower motor, but the design has since been upgraded to further improve airflow.

but also run 13s with a daily-driven 2001 ZX3. While likely much more common by the time this sees print, not many Foci were running heads-up with stock Mustang GTs at the time of the project.

It is the high-horsepower supercharged motors that really benefit from installing a larger throttle body. This particular supercharged motor also featured a ported head, mild Crane cams and long-tube headers. Additional mods included a Focus Sport off-road pipe, Borla exhaust system and adjustable cam sprockets. Naturally the big power producer was the prototype Jackson Racing supercharger featuring a larger M62 blower. It might be possible to just reach 200 wheel horsepower with a modified motor and the smaller M45, but life is so much easier with the larger supercharger. Mounted in front of the blower, the stock throttle body, originally designed

to feed the airflow needs of a 130-hp normally aspirated motor, was expected to supply the necessary air to support twice that power level. Naturally, the stock throttle body was unable to flow sufficient air to support 220 wheel horsepower. Adding the larger 65mm throttle body from Focus Central resulted in an increase of 12-13 horsepower at the wheels. Note that the power gains increased with engine speed. Given that the airflow demands increased with engine speed, this was not surprising. Expect the same gains with a wild naturally aspirated Zetec of equivalent power.

Test 3
Stock versus 65mm Throttle Body (Turbocharged Zetec)

This test illustrates an important point about airflow. The two previous tests illustrated that the power gains offered by a larger (65mm) throttle body vary with airflow. As the power level of the motor increases, so does the airflow demand. An increase in the airflow demand will result in a need for more airflow through the throttle body. At some power level beyond stock, the factory throttle body becomes a restriction. This was illustrated by the power gains offered when we installed the throttle body on the heavily modified normally aspirated motor as well as the supercharged version. In both instances, the power level produced by the Zetec motor was much greater than stock. Note that the additional airflow offered by the Focus Central 65mm throttle body was of little benefit to the near-stock motor. This is because the stock throttle body offered sufficient flow to feed the needs of the near-stock motor.

If the benefits of the 65mm throttle body are determined by the power output of the motor, why didn't the power improve when tested on the turbo motor? While the turbo motor produced slightly more power than the supercharged motor, the power output did not change after we installed the 65mm throttle body. The reason that the larger throttle body did not improve the power output is because the boost pressure sup-

Test 3: Since the stock throttle body was restrictive to the 200-hp supercharged motor, shouldn't that same thing happen on a 200-hp turbo motor?

plied by the F-Max turbo artificially increased the flow capacity of the stock throttle body. Remember that the throttle body was mounted in front of the supercharger, where the blower was forced to draw all of the necessary air for the motor through the throttle opening. By contrast, the throttle body is pressurized in the turbo system. It is this pressure that allows the stock throttle body to flow significantly more than it would without the boost. At the power level tested, the stock throttle body pressurized at 10 psi was able to flow sufficient air to feed the 227-hp Zetec motor.

Test 3: It was necessary to port-match the opening on the stock intake to match the 65mm opening on the throttle body. Even this didn't seem improve the power offered by the 65mm throttle body on the turbo motor. Since the turbo motor forced air through the throttle body, the stock throttle body was not much of a restriction at the 227-hp level. Things might be different at elevated power levels, but we have made over 270 hp using the stock throttle body on a turbo application.

Test 3: Stock vs. 65mm Throttle Body (Turbocharged Zetec)

Engine Specifications

Block:	Stock
Crank:	Stock
Rods:	Stock
Pistons:	Stock
Head:	Focus Central ported
Valves:	tock
Cams:	Crane 210/206
Sprockets:	Focus Central
Intake:	Modified Zetec (Focus Central)
Throttle body:	Stock vs. 65mm
Air intake:	F-Max
Filter:	Cone
Maf:	ProM
Header:	F-Max Turbo Manifold
Exhaust:	Borla
Injectors:	36 lbs./hr.
Turbo:	F-Max
Boost level:	10 psi
Management:	Stock ECU
Fuel pump:	Stock
Intercooler:	F-Max air-to-air

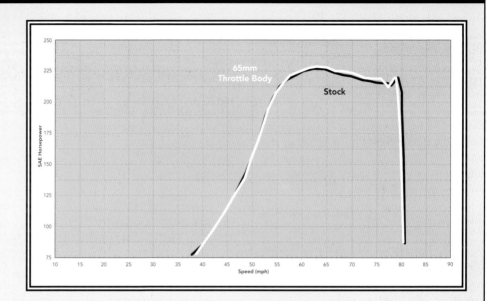

The power level alone is not the determining factor when it comes to throttle body effectiveness. Since the air was being pushed through the throttle body and not pulled, as was the case with the supercharger, the stock throttle body was more than enough for this 225-hp turbo motor.

Test 4
Killer Bee Racing Adjustable Intake (Mild NA motor)

This test demonstrates the effect of changes in intake runner length. More than any other single component (including the camshaft), the intake manifold, and more specifically the intake runner length, determines the effective operating range of the motor. Basically, the runner length determines where the motor will make peak power and what the shape of the power curve will be on both sides of that peak. Sure, other factors contribute to the overall power, but chop a ton of runner length off and watch the torque production plummet.

Test 4: The intake featured slip-fit tubing to facilitate quick changes on the dyno. The manifold was done only as a test piece to determine the optimum length.

Test 4: The author designed this adjustable intake manifold to test the effects of runner length.

Test 4: Installed on the Zetec motor, the adjustable runners altered the power curve significantly.

Basically speaking, long intake runners promote low-rpm power, while short runners promote high-rpm power. The stock Zetec intake features extremely long runners, measuring nearly 18 inches. Compared to, say, a Honda VTEC intake, which measures roughly 12 inches, the Zetec intake was designed to promote low-speed torque production. This is evident in the fact that the stock Zetec motor produces peak power at just 5,400 rpm. By comparison, a short-runner Honda VTEC motor will produce peak power some 2,000 rpm later.

Recognizing the important role the intake plays on the power curve, the author built a custom intake system that featured adjustable runner length. This

Test 4: Killer Bee Racing
Adjustable Intake (Mild NA motor)

Engine Specifications

Block:	Stock
Crank:	Stock
Rods:	Stock
Pistons:	Stock
Head:	Stock
Valves:	Stock
Cams:	Stock
Sprockets:	Stock
Intake:	Stock
Throttle body:	Stock
Air intake:	Custom 3-inch
Filter:	Cone
Maf:	ProM
Header:	Stock
Exhaust:	Stock
Injectors:	Stock
Turbo:	NA
Blower:	NA
Boost level:	NA
Management:	Stock ECU
Fuel pump:	Stock
Intercooler:	NA
Nitrous:	No

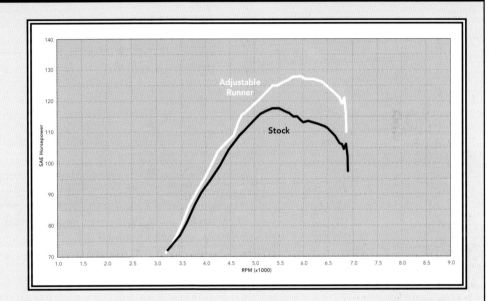

Building an adjustable runner intake manifold took some time, but the results were worth the effort. The optimum runner length was worth 13-15 horsepower over the stock intake, with very little loss in low-speed power.

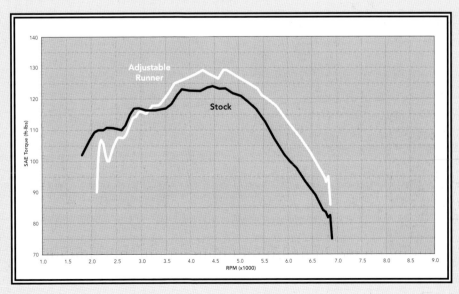

A number of different runner lengths were tried, which produced different power curves.

The optimum runner length lost a minor amount of power below 3,000 rpm, but offered big gains from there up to redline.

Test 5: Intake Shoot-Out: Stock vs. Modified vs. Ford Racing vs. Fabricated vs. Adjustable

Engine Specifications

Block:	Stock
Crank:	Stock
Rods:	Stock
Pistons:	Stock
Head:	Focus Central ported
Valves:	Stock
Cams:	Crane 210/206
Sprockets:	Focus Central
Intake:	Stock vs. Modified, Ford Racing, Fabricated & Adjustable
Throttle body:	65mm
Air intake:	F-Max
Filter:	Cone
Maf:	ProM
Header:	F-Max Turbo Manifold
Exhaust:	Borla
Injectors:	36 lbs./hr.
Turbo:	F-Max
Boost level:	9 psi
Management:	Stock ECU
Fuel pump:	Stock
Intercooler:	F-Max air-to-air

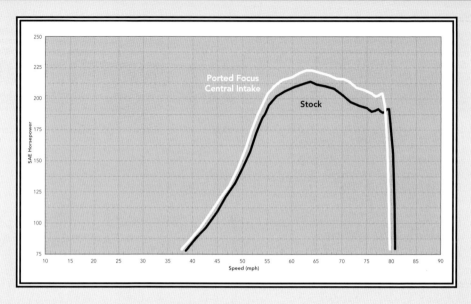

The Focus Central modified 2000 Zetec manifold was worth a solid 10 hp over the stock intake, with no loss in low-speed power.

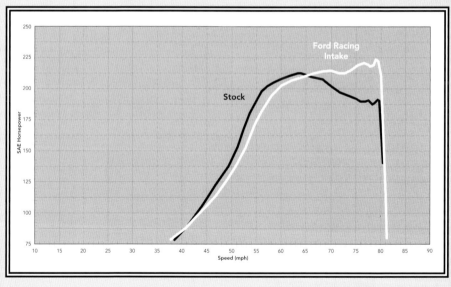

The Ford Racing intake offered additional power past 5500 rpm, but suffered slightly at lower engine speeds.

All of the testing was run on this F-Max turbo motor.

allowed tuning of the power curve to suit different engine configurations. Using slip-fit tubing, the runner length could be adjusted from a minimum of 6 inches to a maximum of 16 inches. Once a length was chosen, the slip fit tubing was taped together using duct tape. Not exactly ideal for street use, but the slip-fit tubing and tape performed perfectly during testing and allowed an ideal runner length to be chosen for both normally aspirated and turbocharged Zetec configurations. The three lines in the graph indicate three different runner lengths chosen during testing. The highest torque production was achieved with the longest runner, with the two other curves produced by respectively shorter runners. Note that the shorter runners offered slightly more power after the power peak, but that the peak values

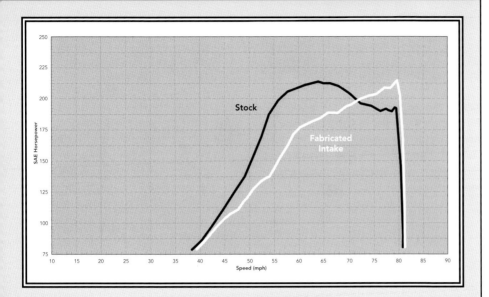

Designed for a high-rpm application, the fabricated sheet-metal intake gained power over the stock intake at the very end of the rev range.

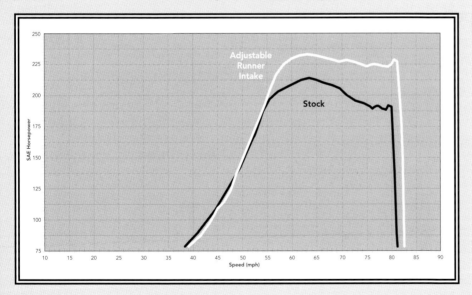

The adjustable runner intake offered improved power over the stock manifold, with only a slight trade off in spool-up.

were identical. The change in runner length shifted the power peak by some 500 rpm, but in each case, the motor produced 130 wheel horsepower. Given wilder cam timing and even greater changes in runner length, it is possible to shift the power peaks even further.

Test 5
Intake Shoot-Out: Stock vs. Modified vs. Ford Racing vs. Fabricated vs. Adjustable

Like the adjustable runner length, this test illustrates what happens when you significantly alter the intake manifold design. The modified Zetec test motor was set up with an F-Max turbo kit. The waste gate was adjusted to provide 9 psi to each intake. The F-Max turbo kit included an air-to-air intercooler, something helpful in keeping the charge temperature down when running over 10 psi of boost. We also made sure to fill the fuel tank with a mixture of premium unleaded and race fuel to absolutely eliminate any chance of detonation. All of the intake manifolds were equipped with a 65mm throttle body, although later testing would illustrate that the larger throttle body was of limited value on the turbo motor at this power level. The motor was run on the chassis dyno with the stock Zetec intake to establish a baseline. The only modifications to the stock motor were port-matching the entry to accept the larger throttle body. Testing has shown that port-matching the intake was worth no power when run alone. Running 9 psi and equipped with the stock intake, the Zetec motor produced a peak of 214 horsepower. Backup runs duplicated the power curve exactly.

The first intake to be tested on the turbo motor was a ported and modified version from a 2000 Zetec motor. According to the experts at Focus Central, the early (2000) intake flows slightly better than the later versions. The 2000 intake was modified by through-porting, which included some epoxy work to produce better entries and improve overall runner flow. According to Dennis Hilliard at Focus Central, the modified intake flows some 25 cfm better than a stock 2001-up version. The

Test 5: The Ford Racing intake offered significant power gains at higher rpm, but the installation required slotting the mounting holes, fabricating an adapter pad for the throttle body, and grinding for alternator clearance.

Test 5: Focus Central supplied a modified 2000 intake that featured porting. This intake was worth a solid 10 hp over the stock intake.

flow improvements made themselves known, as the modified intake increased the power output everywhere, from 2000 rpm all the way to 6500 rpm. Note that the two power curves were other-

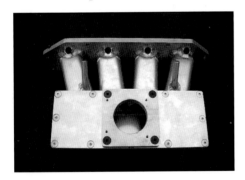

Test 5: This fabricated sheet metal intake illustrated what happens when you dramatically shorten the runner length. The intake lost big power to the stocker, but showed real improvements near redline.

Test 5: The adjustable runner intake performed well thanks to the adjustability. After finding the optimum length for the combination, the adjustable intake bettered the stock intake by a significant margin.

wise identical, a fact dictated by the runner length. The increase in airflow improved the power output, but did not increase the engine speed where the motor made peak power. The added airflow simply elevated the curve.

The next intake tested was from Ford Racing. Unlike the modified stock intake, the Ford Racing unit represented a dramatic change in nearly every design criteria. The Ford Racing intake featured high-flow runners that were both shorter in length and larger in cross section. The Ford Racing intake also featured greater plenum volume compared to the stock intake, no doubt done to further aid top-end performance. Though the design looked promising for a motor equipped with suitable cams and RPM ability, the installation was difficult. Apparently the Ford Racing intake was designed for the ZX2 cylinder head, as the bolt pattern and intake ports did not line up with the ZX3 head. Extensive modifications (including grinding, and reorienting the alternator), eventually allowed us to mount the Ford Racing piece. As expected, the shorter (high-volume) runners shifted the power peak from 5,500 rpm to 6,500 rpm. The Ford Racing intake improved the peak power output from 214 hp to 223 hp, but the gains were as great as 32 horsepower out near 6,500 rpm. Given wilder cam timing and the desire to wind a turbo motor out past 7,000 rpm, the Ford Racing intake might be a good choice if the installation wasn't such a nightmare.

Test intake number 3 was a fabricated sheet-metal piece. The sheet-metal intake featured even shorter runners than the Ford Racing intake, combined with a similar sized plenum. Looking all the world like a true race intake, we suspected that the intake would be somewhat out of place on the mild street motor, especially given the factory rev limiter. This fabricated sheet metal intake test clearly demonstrated the reason why race intakes have no place on street motors, even turbocharged ones. Whether normally aspirated or equipped with forced induction (turbo or supercharged), intake runner length still determines the shape of the power curve. Compared to the stock intake, the turbo motor produced the same peak power number with the short-runner sheet metal intake (214 hp vs 214 hp). The short runner intake shifted the power peak from 5,500 rpm all the way out to 6,700 rpm (the highest RPM run during the test). Judging by the shape of the power curve, the fabricated intake wanted to make peak power well past our shut-down point of 6,700 rpm. Shifting the power curve so dramatically resulted in a dramatic loss in low-speed power. The short runner intake lost as much as 50 wheel horsepower down below 4,000 rpm.

The final turbo intake tested was the author's own adjustable-runner intake. Naturally the runner length was optimized for the test, while the larger ports offered improved flowed compared to the stock manifold. As expected, the greater flow offered a significant power gain. The peak power registered with the adjustable–runner intake was 234 horsepower, a gain of 20 horsepower peak to peak. Out near 6,500 rpm, the gains were as high as 38-40 horsepower. Note that unlike the sheet metal intake, which offered a significant reduction in runner length, the adjustable-runner intake traded very little low-speed power for the big gains past 4,800 rpm. As the turbo spooled up, the adjustable runner intake lagged behind the stock intake, but only by a few horsepower. It is doubtful that this minor loss would be noticeable, either in the seat of the pants or at the track. The gains of 20 peak horsepower

Test 6: SVT Intake & Long Runners vs. Short Runner Length (NA Zetec)

Engine Specifications

Block:	Stock
Crank:	Stock
Rods:	Eagle Forged
Pistons:	JE Forged 8.5:1
Head:	Focus Central (extensively) ported
Valves:	1mm oversize
Cams:	Crower Custom 242/242
Intake:	SVT
Throttle body:	Stock SVT
Air intake:	Custom
Filter:	Cone
Maf:	ProM
Header:	Focus Central Long Tube
Exhaust:	Borla
Injectors:	36 lbs./hr.
Turbo:	NA
Blower:	NA
Boost level:	NA
Management:	Stock ECU
Fuel pump:	Stock
Intercooler:	NA
Nitrous:	No

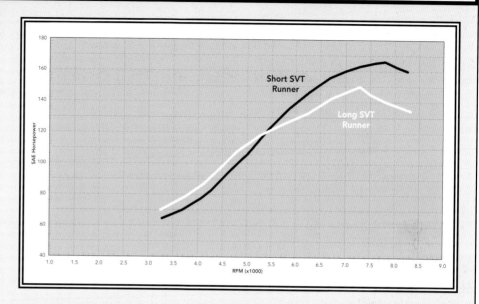

Running the SVT intake on the Zetec proved interesting. As expected, the long runners produced more low-speed power while the short runners produced better top-end power.

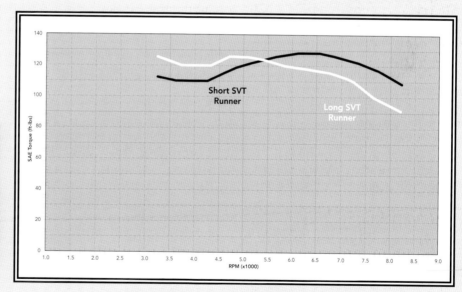

These torque curves illustrate why SVT opted for the dual-runner intake in the first place. Combining the long & short runners broadened the torque curve.

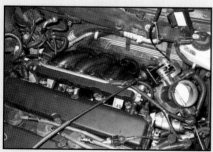

Is this the only SVT-equipped Zetec in the country? Probably not, but it was an interesting experiment.

and 38-40 elsewhere in the curve could most certainly be felt behind the wheel. The gains would also result in a dramatic improvement in 1/4-mile times. This test shows that the right intake can make all the difference in the world.

Test 6
SVT Intake & Long Runners vs Short Runner Length (NA Zetec)

Obviously Ford recognized the influence of intake runner length on power production. Knowing that long runners promote low-speed torque while short runners produce exceptional top-end horsepower, Ford saw fit to combine the two systems into one. Okay, maybe they took the idea from

Test 6: After the release of the SVT version, I immediately wanted one of the dual-runner intakes. Check out the difference between the SVT version and the Zetec intake.

the Acura Integra GSR, but the SVT Focus features a trick dual-runner intake that allows the motor to run on long runners at lower engine speeds and switch over to shorter runners at a pre-determined engine speed. Providing two distinct runner lengths allows the motor to produce a broader power curve. This is especially true on the Honda VTEC motor when combined with a pair of cam profiles to match the power curves of the intake runners. The SVT intake works by rotating a section of additional runner length into position, then allowing it to rotate away at a given engine speed. Rotating the runner section away effectively shortens the runner length, allowing the SVT motor to produce not only peak power at 7,000 rpm, but also a nice, flat, torque curve.

For this test, we decided to install the SVT intake on a modified Zetec motor to demonstrate the effect of the changes in runner length offered by the SVT intake. The game plan included run-

ning the modified Zetec motor from 2,000 rpm to 7,500 rpm (the factory rev limiter was removed) with each of the two runner lengths offered by the SVT manifold. By overlaying the two graphs, we could determine the cross-over point of the respective power curves. The cross-over point determines the ideal engine speed to switch from the long runner to the short runner—thus producing the best overall power curve. The motor was first run with the long runner section in place. The modified Zetec motor produced 149 hp at 7,000 rpm. We then repeated the test after rotating the long-runner section out of the way. This allowed the motor to breathe through the short runner length. Not the drop in power from 3,000 rpm to 5,400 rpm. The cross-over point occurred at 5,500 rpm, thus if we were to install the SVT intake on this modified motor, the ideal switch-over point would be 5,400 rpm. This switch-over point would give us all the low-speed power offered by the long runners with all the top-end power offered by the short runners, with none of the trade-offs.

Test 7
Stock vs. Jackson Racing Intake
Effect of Runner Length

While testing a Jackson Racing supercharger kit on a ZX3, we noticed something interesting on the power curve. Installing the Jackson Racing supercharger kit improved the power output (as expected), but adding the

Test 7: Both the stock and 65mm throttle bodies were tried (no power difference), but the real test was the dramatic change in runner length. The short-runner intake shifted the peak horsepower production by 1,000 rpm, losing low-speed power in the process. Short-runner intakes are not ideal for street motors.

Test 7: While running tests on the Jackson Racing supercharger, the author questioned the effect of the short runner intake. The JR intake offered only 2-inch runners compared to the 18-inch runners on the stock Zetec intake.

blower also altered the overall shape of the curve. Knowing that the presence of (street-level) boost does not usually make a major change in the shape of the curve, we looked elsewhere for the culprit. Our search brought us to the intake manifold, as the Jackson Racing kit featured a dedicated intake casting to allow mounting the blower. The new intake manifold featured dramatically shorter runners than the stock intake, but only a test would show if our suspicions were correct. To accurately test the effect of the change in runner length offered by the revised intake casting, we needed to separate the intake manifold and blower and test them separately.

Test 6: On the dyno, the two runner lengths demonstrated why the SVT version has such a broad power band. The long runners produced better low-speed torque, while the short runners improved top-end power.

Test 7: Stock vs. Jackson Racing Intake
Effect of Runner Length

Engine Specifications

Block:	Stock
Crank:	Stock
Rods:	Stock
Pistons:	Stock
Head:	Stock
Valves:	Stock
Cams:	Stock
Sprockets:	Stock
Intake:	Stock
Throttle body:	Stock
Air intake:	Stock Ford Escape
Filter:	JR cone
Maf:	Stock
Header:	Stock
Exhaust:	Stock
Injectors:	Stock
Turbo:	NA
Blower:	Jackson Racing
Boost level:	5 psi
Management:	Stock ECU
Fuel pump:	Stock
Intercooler:	NA
Nitrous:	No

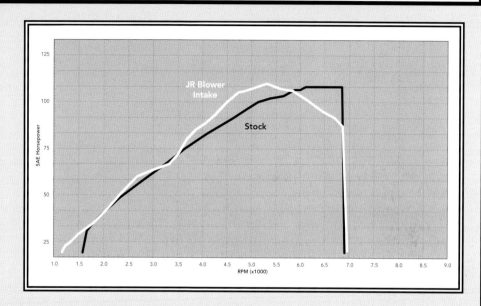

Testing the short-runner intake supplied with the Jackson Racing supercharger kit in normally aspirated form resulted in a significant drop in power up to 5,750 rpm. The long-runner stock intake did much better.

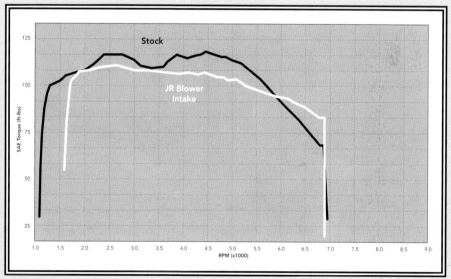

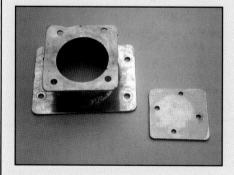

The author's crew chief Jason "Jay Dub" Wilson fabricated this adapter to mount the Zetec throttle body on the Jackson Racing blower intake without the supercharger.

The short-runner intake produced a flat torque curve, but note that the curve did not trail off as dramatically as did the motor equipped with the stock intake. We would like to see the power curve of the motor with the blower and the stock long-runner intake to provide the best of both worlds.

We decided to run the test motor with the blower manifold in normally aspirated configuration (without the supercharger). To do this, we installed the blower intake and then fabricated an adapter plate to mount the stock throttle body to the Jackson Racing intake. This allowed us to run the short-runner blower intake without the blower. The motor was then run with the blower and then again with the stock intake. By running the motor in the three configurations, we

Test 8: Focus Central Composite vs.
Ford Racing Intake — Wild Turbo Zetec

Engine Specifications

Block:	Stock
Crank:	Stock
Rods:	Eagle
Pistons:	JE Forged
Head:	Ported
Valves:	1mm Oversized
Cams:	Custom Crower
Sprockets:	Focus Central Adj
Intake:	Focus Central Composite vs Ford Racing
Throttle body:	65mm
Air intake:	Custom 4-inch
Filter:	K&N Cone
Maf:	None
Header:	Innovative Turbo
Exhaust:	None
Injectors:	72 lbs./hr.
Turbo:	Innovative Turbo GT66
Blower:	NA
Boost level:	26 psi
Management:	Pectel ECU
Fuel pump:	Aeromotive
Intercooler:	Vortech Aftercooler

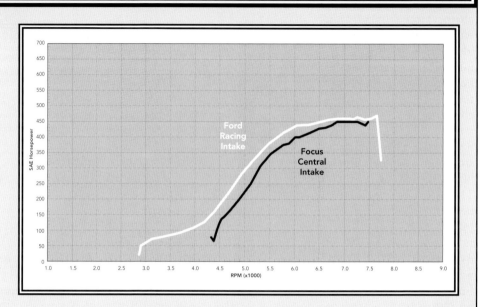

Long runners produce better low and mid-range power. The long runners in the Ford Racing intake improved the power output of this turbo motor compared to the short-runner custom composite intake.

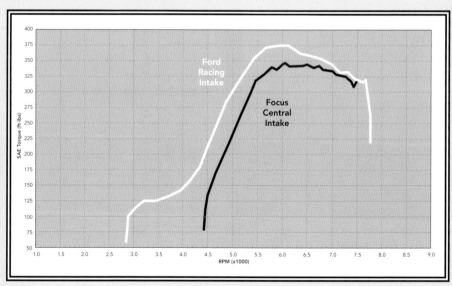

The gain in torque offered by the longer runners was huge. The long-runner intake offered 50 additional ft-lbs from 4,500 rpm to 5,500 rpm.

The cast aluminum Ford Racing intake was used on the 500-hp turbo motor with great success.

could determine not only the change offered by the short-runner intake, but also the power offered by the supercharger itself. Basically, what was the intake worth and what was the boost worth? Equipped with the stock intake, the Zetec motor produced 109 horsepower at the wheels. Once we installed the Jackson Racing blower intake and fabricated throttle body adapter, the motor produced an identical 109 wheel horsepower. Though the two intakes produced the same peak power, the curves were dramatically different. The short-runner intake produced peak power at 6,250 rpm, 1,000 rpm higher than with the stock intake. Given the higher peak power engine speed, the short-runner intake lost power compared to the stock intake from idle to 5,600 rpm.

Adding the blower to the mix naturally improved the power output of the motor, but more importantly (for this chapter), the curves produced with and without the supercharger were nearly identical. This illustrates the fact that the intake design (and not the presence of boost) was responsible for determining the shape of the power curve. If you check out the curve of the supercharged motor in Chapter 6 (Test 1), you will notice that the power curve with the stock intake effectively splits the non-blown and supercharged power curves. The ideal combination would probably be a supercharger combined with the long runners of the stock intake. Unfortunately, available space limits the effective runner length that can be combined with the blower. This test correlates the findings achieved with the intakes tested on the turbo motor. Whether supercharged, turbocharged, or normally aspirated, the intake runner length should be chosen to produce the most effective power band in the desire rpm range. High-rpm race motors will need short runners while most street motors will run best with longer runners.

Test 8
Focus Central Composite vs. Ford Racing Intake Wild Turbo Zetec

The wild turbo Zetec combination was used in a number of tests for this book, including a comparison between two different intake manifolds. The intake comparison centered on a short-runner composite intake built by Focus Central and the long(er)-runner cast aluminum intake offered by Ford Racing. Once again it bears mentioning that the Ford Racing intake required extensive modifications before it could be successfully bolted in place to the ported Zetec head. Though the mounting holes for the Ford Racing intake are in the correct location, bolting on the head using the supplied bolt holes positioned the intake ports incorrectly. The cure was to slot the mounting holes to properly orient the intake manifold ports relative to the

cylinder head. It will also be necessary to grind some material off the underside of port 4 for alternator clearance, as well as fabricating an adapter plate for the throttle body (the Ford Racing mounting holes were not designed for a Zetec throttle body). Speaking of throttle bodies, both manifolds were run with the same 65mm throttle body from Focus Central.

The test motor was a modified 2.0L Zetec featuring a ported head, custom Crower cams, and a Sean Hyland short block. The motor was equipped with an Innovative Turbo system including a GT66 turbo. Vortech supplied one of their very efficient air-to-water After Coolers for our testing. Boost for the turbo motor was controlled by an Innovative waste gate and APEXi Super AVC, allowing up to 2 bar of boost. Equipped with the short-runner composite intake, the motor produced 453 horsepower at 7,400 rpm and 346 ft-lbs of torque at 6,000 rpm. After swapping on the Ford Racing intake, the peak power increased slightly to 463 hp, while torque was up to 374 ft-lbs. Naturally the motor was run at the same boost level for each intake. The real benefit of the long-runner intake was a dramatic improvement in mid-range torque production. The turbo spooled up much

Test 8: This composite intake from Focus Central was optimized for high-rpm power, but torque production suffered compared to the long-runner Ford Racing intake.

quicker with the long-runner intake. Credit the long runners for improving the torque production, something that helped provide an increase in exhaust energy to the turbo, which in turn produced (more) boost pressure at a lower engine speed. When it comes to intake manifolds, always choose the longest runner you can get away with without sacrificing maximum (peak) power. If you want your power peak to be at 6,500 rpm, select the longest intake runner length that still produces peak power at 6,500 rpm. The long runners will provide a much-improved overall power curve.

Test 8: Equipped with the Ford Racing intake, the turbo motor produced 463 hp and (more importantly) 374 ft-lbs of torque at 25 psi.

DEEP BREATHING EXERCISES

HEADS, CAMS & SPROCKETS

When combined with the intake manifold, the cylinder head and cams make up what can be referred to as the Big Three; they are the three most important power production components. Sure, things such as compression, a tubular header, and even the throttle body can help the motor produce power, but the major players in the equation are the intake manifold (runner length), the cylinder head flow, and the cam timing. Naturally it is important that these three subsystems be designed to work together for optimum performance. Working together means that they are designed to produce power in the same effective rpm

The cam profiles, sprockets and head flow all play a critical part in optimum performance.

range. By this we mean that the intake runner length should be sized to maximize power in the same rpm range as the cam timing (specifically, the duration). It wouldn't do much good to have a set of cams that want to rev cleanly to 8,000 rpm only to choke them off with an intake designed to make peak power at 5,500 rpm. The result would be a motor that makes very little low-speed power thanks to the wild cam timing and no top-end power because of the excessive runner length. Naturally the cylinder head flow must be sufficient to feed the airflow needs of the motor at the intended operating range.

The stock 2.0L Zetec motor was designed to produce peak horsepower at 5,400 rpm. The relatively low (rpm) power peak has several effects on the overall power curve. Ford intentionally designed the Zetec motor to provide immediate throttle response. After all, the Focus was designed primarily as a commuter and not a dedicated race car. The Zetec features long intake runners designed to promote low-speed power production. The long runners are one of the reasons the motor revs to 5,500 rpm and then falls off sharply thereafter. The power curve is also a function of the mild cam timing and relatively small intake and exhaust ports in the cylinder head. In a sense, the power curve was designed to provide the illusion of a high-performance motor by offering surprising throttle response and impressive (for its displacement) torque production. Unfortunately, when pressed into serious performance duty, the combination soon runs out of steam. Usually this happens just as the competitor's VTEC cams kick in. That slight advantage you had from all the torque soon disappears and the VTEC boys motor off into the sunset.

Naturally the cure to the low-speed Zetec blues is to modify the Big Three performance components. The intake choices were covered in chapter 2. Improving the cylinder head (Base, Zetec or even SVT) is simply a matter of porting to improve the airflow. It is important to note that improving the airflow of a cylinder head is tricky business. Assuming you even know how to utilize

Test 1: Even on stock motors, the cam timing can be off from the factory.

Test 1: The stock Zetec cam sprockets are not adjustable.

porting tools, you can't just go after the port with a grinder and hog it out. In this case, bigger is not the desired route to better. Improving the airflow without sacrificing low-lift flow (important both for low-speed power and average airflow) is difficult. Getting an intake or exhaust port to flow more air is easy, but getting the improvements at all flow lift numbers is much more difficult. Naturally the difficult route is the best way to improve power. At the time of this writing, Focus Central had managed to improve the airflow of a Zetec cylinder head by more than 50 cfm per runner. This is an amazing amount considering the fact that the stock (intake) port flowed less than 200 cfm. Even more impressive is that the high-lift gains were achieved without sacrificing low-lift flow. As a very general rule of thumb, if you take the flow in cfm (measured at 28 inches) of one intake port, that will equal the power potential of a 4-cylinder motor. Naturally this is a rough estimate, as a great many variables also influence the eventual output of the motor.

While the head flow can determine how much power is possible, the cam timing works with the intake runner length to determine where the power will be made. One need only look at the dual-cam VTEC systems employed by Honda/Acura to see the effect of cam timing on power production. The VTEC system employs two cam profiles for each pair of valves. During normal operation, each pair of intake or exhaust valves is operated by a pair of followers

riding on the low-speed cam lobes. A third follower between the other two rides on a more radical cam lobe, designed for high-rpm use. At a predetermined point, oil pressure engages a pin that locks the high-rpm follower to the other two, so that the motor runs on the wilder cam profile. This way, the VTEC motor can run on the mild primary cam lobes for maximum fuel economy and reduced emissions, while the wilder VTEC cam lobes offer exceptional high-rpm power.

Unfortunately, the Zetec Focus motor is not so equipped and must rely on a single cam profile. It is for this reason that any motor not equipped with a VTEC-type system will always be somewhat of a compromise in terms of power production. The cam timing will dictate the effective operating range of the motor. When it comes to a broad power curve, one cam profile is obviously not as effective as two.

Like the runner length of an intake manifold, the cam timing will effectively shift the torque curve. Installing mild cam profiles can actually improve power across the rev range compared to the stock cams, but eventually it will become necessary to trade low-speed power for power higher in the rev range. The Crower Stage 4 cams used in the 12-second Focus Central motor (see Chapter 9, Engine Build-Ups) are a perfect example of this. A stock motor makes peak torque at 4,500 rpm. Installing the Stage 4 Crower cams (along with a short-runner intake and extensively ported head)

Test 1: Stock vs. AEM Adjustable Cam Sprockets (Stock NA Zetec)

Engine Specifications

Block:	Stock
Crank:	Stock
Rods:	Stock
Pistons:	Stock
Head:	Stock
Valves:	Stock
Cams:	Stock
Sprockets:	Stock vs AEM
Intake:	Stock
Throttle body:	Stock
Air intake:	AEM
Filter:	AEM cone
Maf:	AEM
Header:	Stock
Exhaust:	Stock
Injectors:	Stock
Turbo:	NA
Blower:	NA
Boost level:	NA
Management:	Stock ECU
Fuel pump:	Stock
Intercooler:	NA
Nitrous:	No

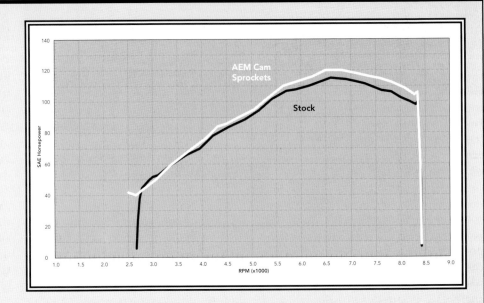

It took some time adjusting the AEM cam sprockets, but it was worth it as we were able to gain as much as 5-6 horsepower.

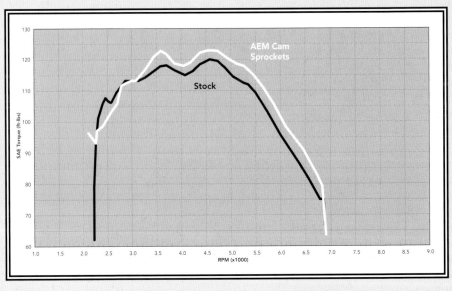

The proper cam timing resulted in a significant torque gain across the rev range.

These AEM sprockets allowed adjustments of the cam timing to increase performance.

shifted the torque peak to 5,700 rpm. The horsepower peak was also shifted, from 5,500 rpm to 8,400 rpm, where the 2.0L (stock short block) produced 223 horsepower at the wheels. While that particular motor required a great many components to exceed 220 wheel horsepower, the cams were a major part of the power production. The downside to wilder cam timing will usually be a loss in low-speed power. For most street motors, especially those retaining the long factory intake, stick with milder cam profiles than the Crower Stage 4s. Look for something with no more than 220-230 degrees of duration at .050.

Test 1
Stock versus AEM Adjustable Cam Sprockets (Stock NA Zetec)

Adjustable cam sprockets can greatly improve the power output of a motor, but should be considered more of a tuning tool than an outright power

Test 2: It took several hours to run through all of the adjustments on the cam sprockets. Sometimes it is worthwhile and other times it is just an exercise in frustration.

enhancement. The reason for this is that adjusting the cam sprockets can hurt power just as easily as help it. Adjustable cam sprockets can only be used to advance and retard the lobe separation angle of the intake and exhaust cams. The sprockets will have no effect on lift or duration (though adjusting the cams can increase overlap), or the time that both the intake and exhaust valves are open in the cycle. This overlap phenomenon can be used to increase cylinder filling by pulling the intake charge into the cylinder. Unfortunately, too much of a good thing can be bad, and that suction created by the exhaust flow can literally suck the intake charge right out the open exhaust valve. How and when this occurs is dictated by the cam timing, overlap and the engine speed. Excessive overlap can create havoc at low engine speeds, where there is plenty of time for the intake charge to escape out the open exhaust valve, but limiting the time available for the intake air to travel (by increasing engine speed) can produce optimum results, thus adjusting this overlap is rpm specific.

It is a very general rule that advancing a cam will help improve low-speed power, while retarding a cam will increase top-end power. These rules are application specific, as we have seen the reverse be true on some wild combinations. It should be noted that changing cam timing should be done one gear at a time, and in small increments. Naturally, this is a procedure best left for the dyno.

Adjust one cam at a time starting with the intake, and test the power gains or losses. When adjustments in one direction start to reduce power, try the opposite direction. Once you have maxed out the power available from the intake cam, start changes to the exhaust cam (following the same procedure). It may be necessary to recheck the intake cam once you have optimized the exhaust cam, as changing one can change the needs of the other. On our stock Zetec motor, adjusting the cams sprockets was worth an additional 5-6 horsepower, due in no small part to the fact that stock cam sprockets can be so far off from the factory.

Test 2
Stock versus
Focus Central Cam Sprockets
(JR Supercharged Zetec)

When it comes to maximizing performance of a twin-cam motor, adjustable cam sprockets can make a major difference in performance. While often times beneficial, they are also potentially detrimental to performance. More often than not, adjustable cam sprockets reduce the power output of a given combination or at best, trade power at different rpm points. It is possible to improve the low-speed power but the gains in torque can be offset by a sizable reduction in peak power. Naturally the reverse is also true, where top-end performance is maximized only to dramatically reduce low-speed power. On rare occasions, it is possible to

increase power across the rev range, but figure on spending considerable time of the dyno in search of the hidden power. Don't expect to find a ton of power with installing adjustable cam sprockets on a stock motor, although we have seen stock Zetec cam timing off by more than a few degrees. Adjustable cam sprockets are most beneficial when installing aftermarket cams and/or a milled cylinder head. Milling moves the crank and cam centerlines closer together, requiring adjustments (usually 2 degrees advance per .030-in. milled) to maintain proper valve timing.

The power gains illustrated on the accompanying graph were not the result of a simple back-to-back dyno test. It took 10 dyno runs with cam adjustments coming in 2-degree increments (both advance and retard). It is best to alter the timing of only one cam, starting with the intake first. Try advancing 2 degrees from the 0 mark and then try retarding 2 degrees from the 0 mark. The dyno will indicate which direction your combination likes. If 2 degrees works well, try 2 more. Remember it is always a good idea to run high-octane fuel when testing, as this will eliminate the knock sensor as a power variable (not to mention making things much safer). Once you reach a point where additional cam timing has no effect, try the same procedure with the exhaust cam. Once you find the maximum power from the exhaust cam, go back and retry adjusting the intake cam with the newly posi-

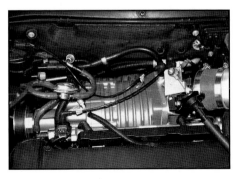

Test 2: Oddly enough, this supercharged motor did not respond to the adjustable cam sprockets. Some combinations are more optimized than others at the factory settings.

Test 3: Wilder engine combinations usually require adjustments to the cam timing. This 2.0L motor featured custom Crower cams, a ported head and a custom composite intake manifold.

Test 2: Stock vs. Focus Central Cam Sprockets
(JR Supercharged Zetec)

Engine Specifications

Block:	Stock
Crank:	Stock
Rods:	Stock
Pistons:	Stock
Head:	Ported
Valves:	Stock
Cams:	Crane Stage 1
Sprockets:	Focus Central Adj
Intake:	JR Blower Intake
Throttle body:	65mm
Air intake:	Custom 3-inch
Filter:	Cone
Maf:	ProM
Header:	Focus Sport Long Tube
Exhaust:	Borla
Injectors:	36 lbs./hr.
Turbo:	NA
Blower:	Jackson Racing M62
Boost level:	10 psi
Management:	Stock ECU
Fuel pump:	Stock
Intercooler:	NA
Nitrous:	No

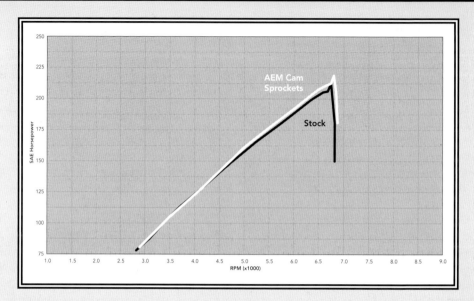

After spending considerable time on the DynoJet, we were rewarded with just 3-4 horsepower. The supercharged combination was just not responsive to changes in cam timing.

These Focus Central adjustable sprockets were employed on the supercharged motor.

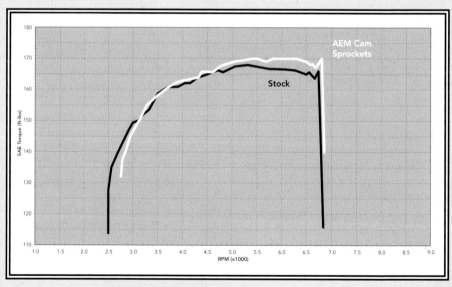

Most of the torque gains occurred past 4,700 rpm.

tioned exhaust cam. Often additional power can come from readjustment of the intake after finalizing the exhaust cam. On our supercharger combination equipped with a milled head and Stage 1 Crane cams, we picked up only 3-4 peak horsepower.

Test 3
Stock versus Focus Central Cam Sprockets (Modified NA Zetec)

While the stock motor responded well to the adjustable cam sprockets, the wilder the combination (especially true of cams), the greater the potential gain from adjustable cam sprockets. The great thing about adjustable sprockets is that the power gains can come at low, medium and even high engine speeds.

Sometimes it's necessary to trade low-speed power for top-end power, in much the same way as wild cam timing or short-runner intakes trade power. Occasionally, your combination will respond well to the changes in cam timing and the power will increase across the board. Our modified 2.0L Zetec test motor (actually the 500-hp turbo motor prior to installing the turbo) responded well to both intake and exhaust cam sprocket adjustments, increasing power at various engine speeds with each adjustment. The custom Crower cams were obviously pretty far removed from stock, so it wasn't surprising that the motor responded so well to the cam sprocket adjustments. The sprockets improved the power output by as much as 12 horsepower and 15 ft-lbs, pretty impressive considering the power was achieved with simple sprockets adjustments.

Test 3: Stock vs. Focus Central Cam Sprockets (Modified NA Zetec)

Engine Specifications

Block:	Stock
Crank:	Stock
Rods:	Eagle
Pistons:	Forged
Head:	Ported
Valves:	1 mm oversize
Cams:	Custom Crower
Sprockets:	Focus Central Adj
Intake:	Focus Central Composite
Throttle body:	65mm
Air intake:	Custom 3-inch
Filter:	Cone
Maf:	ProM
Header:	Focus Central Long Tube
Exhaust:	Borla
Injectors:	Stock
Turbo:	NA
Blower:	NA
Boost level:	NA
Management:	Stock ECU
Fuel pump:	Stock
Intercooler:	NA
Nitrous:	No

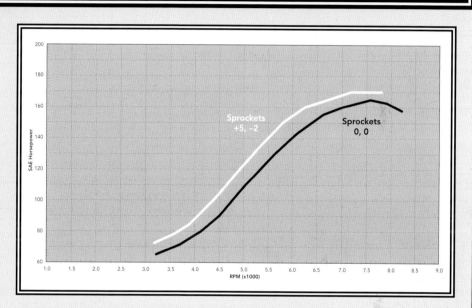

Modified motors usually respond well to cam timing changes, and this 2.0L Zetec was no exception.

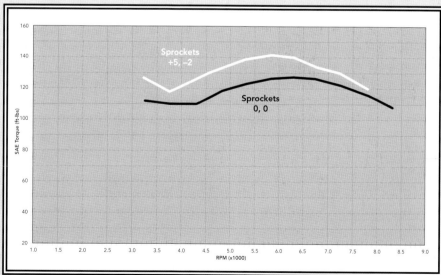

On the Focus Central chassis dyno, the modified Zetec picked up 12 horsepower and 15 ft-lbs of torque.

The adjustable cam sprockets offered significant power gains, to the tune of 12 hp and 15 ft-lbs of torque.

Test 3: Adjustments to the Focus Central cam sprockets resulted in significant power gains on this modified Zetec motor.

Test 4
Stock versus AEM Cam Sprockets (Turbocharged Zetec)

In the previous tests, we illustrated the power gains offered by adjustable sprockets on stock and modified normally aspirated combinations as well as a supercharged Zetec. This test not only

Test 4: This turbo motor was used to demonstrate that it is just as easy to lose power adjusting the cam sprockets as it is to gain power.

Test 4: The AEM cam sprockets were adjusted in 2-degree increments to illustrate what can happen during testing.

includes testing on a turbo motor, but I also made the effort to include some of the power losses available by adjusting the sprockets. Interestingly enough, the cam sprockets were optimized for the normally aspirated motor (5 degrees advance on the intake and 2 degrees retard on the exhaust), but ended up working best on this turbo application. So much for turbo motors always wanting different cam timing than normally aspirated motors. The first test involved changing the cam timing from +5i, -2e to +5i, 0e, or we basically advanced the exhaust cam by 2 degrees. Doing so dropped the power everywhere. The next test involved retarding the exhaust cam further, from –2 degrees to –4 degrees. The result was a drop in mid-range power from 4,000 rpm to 4,800 rpm, though there was no loss above this point. The final test illustrated in the graphs was to reset the exhaust cam to –2 and to retard the intake cam from +5 to +3. Retarding the intake cam 2 degrees resulted in a substantial drop in power, though the low-speed power did not suffer. These tests illustrate what to expect when changing cam timing.

Test 5
Stock versus Focus Central Head Package (Mild NA Zetec)

When it comes to making serious horsepower, no simple bolt-ons are going to get the job done, unless the bolt-ons happen to be nitrous, a turbo or supercharger system. Air intakes, headers, and throttle bodies are all good for additional power on the right appli-

Test 4: The adjustments consistently lost power on this turbo application as the motor was already optimized.

Test 5: The Focus Central head package offered an impressive 30-hp gain over the factory components.

Test 5: The Focus Central head package included dual-pattern Crower cams that favored the intake.

cation, but sometimes 10 or 15 horsepower just isn't enough. When it comes time for serious horsepower, look for a package deal, not unlike the head package offered by Focus Central. Unfortunately for enthusiasts, the power output of the Zetec motor is not limited by one component. Wouldn't it be nice if the throttle body was the limiting factor and all we had to do to gain 25-30 extra horsepower was to install a larger throttle body? Well, in reality, adding serious power requires serious modifications to not just one component but to many. In our case, the many components included the cylinder head, camshafts, and mass air meter (mostly for tuning). The result of replacing all the stock hardware with the ported head, revised cam profiles, and mass air meter was an impressive 30 horsepower at the wheels.

Test 4 : Stock versus AEM Cam Sprockets (Turbocharged Zetec)

Engine Specifications

Block:	Stock
Crank:	Stock
Rods:	Stock
Pistons:	Stock
Head:	Ported
Valves:	Stock
Cams:	Crane Stage 1
Sprockets:	Stock vs. AEM Adj
Intake:	Focus Central Ported 2000
Throttle body:	65mm
Air intake:	Custom 3.5-inch
Filter:	Cone
Maf:	None
Header:	Innovative Turbo
Exhaust:	None
Injectors:	72 lbs./hr.
Turbo:	Innovative T04E-46
Blower:	NA
Boost level:	12 psi
Management:	Pectel
Fuel pump:	Stock w/KB Boost-a-Pump
Intercooler:	Vortech air-to-water Aftercooler
Nitrous:	No

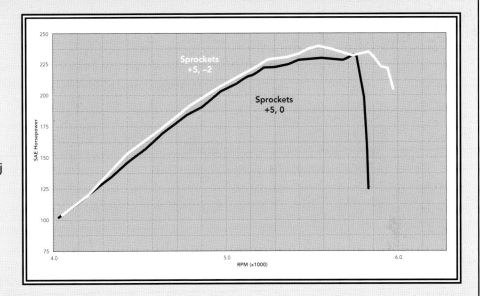

Sometimes adjusting cam sprockets will result in nothing but a loss in power. Advancing the exhaust cam dropped power across the board.

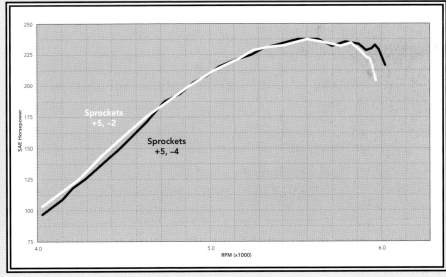

Retarding the intake cam 2 degrees dropped power from 4,200 rpm up.

Retarding the exhaust cam 2 degrees reduced the power output up to 4,700 rpm, but the power remained the same from 4,700 rpm up.

The Focus Central head package included a ported Zetec head that improved the airflow by nearly 30 cfm. Focus Central then added a pair of custom Crower cam profiles that offered more intake lift and duration than exhaust (the reverse of the original Stage 3s). The lift and duration figures were skewed in favor of the intake due to the excellent exhaust flow relative to the intake flow. In addition to the porting and revised cam profiles, the Zetec head also received minor milling to increase the compression ratio. It is important to point out that adjustments to the cam sprockets will be necessary to offset the distance lost through milling. Figure roughly 1.5-2 degrees per .030-inch material removal. The final modification was to install a ProM mass air meter with an Optimizer to tune the combination.

Test 5 : Stock versus Focus Central Head Package (Mild NA Zetec)

Engine Specifications

Block:	Stock
Crank:	Stock
Rods:	Stock
Pistons:	Stock
Head:	tock vs Ported
Valves:	Stock
Cams:	Stock vs Crower Stage 3 in & 2 ex
Sprockets:	Stock vs Focus Central Adj
Intake:	Focus Central ported 2000
Throttle body:	65mm
Air intake:	Focus Central Cold Air
Filter:	Cone
Maf:	Stock vs ProM
Header:	Stock vs Focus Central
Exhaust:	Borla
Injectors:	Stock 19 lbs./hr.
Turbo:	NA
Blower:	NA
Boost level:	NA
Management:	Stock ECU
Fuel pump:	Stock
Intercooler:	NA

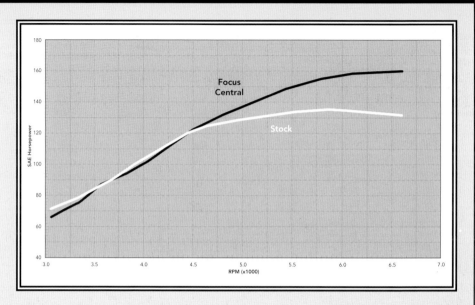

The Focus Central head package offered big-time power gains from 4,750 rpm on up.

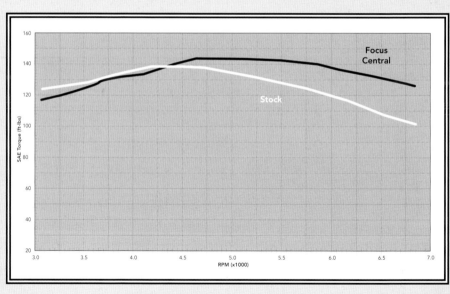

The experts at Focus Central can swap a head in nothing flat.

The slight loss was probably due to the more aggressive cam timing, but check out the extra 30 horsepower near redline.

The motor was previously equipped with a 65mm throttle body, long-tube header and cat-back exhaust. Before the head package, the motor produced 135 hp at 6,000 rpm and 145 ft-lbs at 4,500 rpm. After the mods, the power jumped to 162 hp and the torque to 144 ft-lbs.

Test 6
Stock versus
Focus Central Head Package
(JR Supercharged Zetec)

When it comes to making a great blower motor, the best thing you can do

is start out with a good normally aspirated motor. This test illustrates what happened when we swapped out the stock Zetec cylinder head and cams for a ported head and Crane Stage 1 cams from Focus Central. If you check out the chapter on engine build-ups, the 12-

second Zetec build is a perfect illustration of what is possible using the stock Zetec short block. The modifications were much less extensive in this test, since the only components we changed were the ported cylinder head and Crane cams. The cam swap included a set of Focus Central adjustable cam sprockets to dial in the cams. The cylinder head was also milled slightly to increase the compression ratio, something not normally desirable on a supercharged motor, but our early Focus Central head package was originally planned for a normally aspirated motor. It is also important to note that this particular head package featured minimal porting, in fact, the exhaust ports

Test 6 : Stock versus Focus Central Head Package (JR Supercharged Zetec)

Engine Specifications

Block:	Stock
Crank:	Stock
Rods:	Stock
Pistons:	Stock
Head:	Stock vs Ported
Valves:	Stock
Cams:	Stock vs Crane Stage 1
Sprockets:	Stock vs Focus Central Adj
Intake:	JR Blower Inatke
Throttle body:	65mm
Air intake:	Custom 3-inch
Filter:	Cone
Maf:	ProM
Header:	Focus Central
Exhaust:	Borla
Injectors:	36 lbs./hr.
Turbo:	NA
Blower:	Jackson Racing M62
Boost level:	10 psi
Management:	Stock ECU
Fuel pump:	Stock
Intercooler:	NA
Nitrous:	No

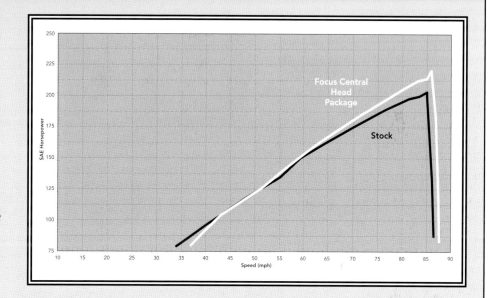

This early example of the Focus Central head package was worth near 20 horsepower on this supercharged Zetec. The head packages now include improved porting and more effective cam profiles.

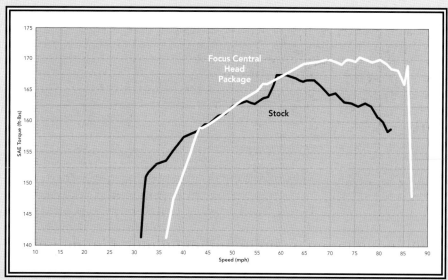

On the dyno, the head package was worth 17-20 horsepower.

The head package did not reduce the power output of the supercharged motor down low, just offered improvements up top.

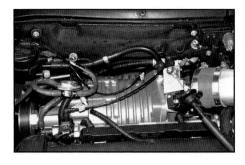

Test 6: Early in the development, the Focus Central head package was applied to the author's supercharged Focus in a quest for additional power.

Test 7: Installing a Focus Central cam sprocket on the exhaust side of the SVT motor resulted in some impressive power gains.

remained untouched. Each cylinder head now features extensive porting of both the intake and exhaust ports as well as larger valves.

The supercharged Zetec motor was run on the DynoJet chassis dyno to establish a baseline with the stock head and cams. The Focus was then driven to Focus Central headquarters where the gang tore into the motor and swapped on the ported head and Crane Stage 1 cams. Dennis Hilliard from Focus Central set up the cylinder head and cams prior to the installation. It is important to set up the valve lash with the new cams, especially when installing new valves and performing a valve job.

Before the head package, the supercharged motor produced 202 horsepower at the wheels. After installing the components from Focus Central, the peak power jumped to 220 hp. As expected, the majority of the power gains came high in the rev range. The added airflow resulted in a slight drop in boost, to the tune of 1/4 to 3/4 psi. Check out the previous head package test (on the normally aspirated motor) to see what is possible with a more extensively ported head.

Test 7
Stock vs Focus Central
Adjustable Sprockets
(Stock SVT Focus)

Unlike the standard Zetec motor, the SVT version is equipped with variable cam timing. The electronic cam timing advances and retards the intake cam according to parameters dictated by the factory computer. The exhaust cam is not equipped with the electronic cam

Test 6: The head package applied to the author's Zetec motor included a mildly ported head, Crane Stage 1 cams and adjustable cam sprockets.

Test 7: Though equipped with electronically adjustable intake cam timing, the exhaust cam timing was stationary.

Test 7: Stock vs Focus Central
Adjustable Sprockets-(Stock SVT Focus)

Engine Specifications

Block:	Stock
Crank:	Stock
Rods:	Stock
Pistons:	Stock
Head:	Stock
Valves:	Stock
Cams:	Stock
Sprockets:	Stock vs Focus Central Adj
Intake:	Stock SVT
Throttle body:	Stock SVT
Air intake:	Custom 3-inch
Filter:	Cone
Maf:	Stock
Header:	Focus Central
Exhaust:	SVT
Injectors:	Stock
Turbo:	NA
Blower:	NA
Boost level:	NA
Management:	Stock ECU
Fuel pump:	Stock
Intercooler:	NA
Nitrous:	No

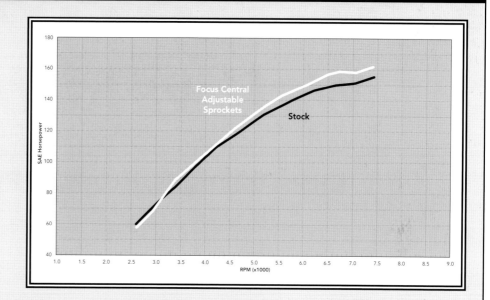

Installing an adjustable exhaust cam sprocket on the SVT (equipped with electronic intake cam timing) resulted in a nice power gain.

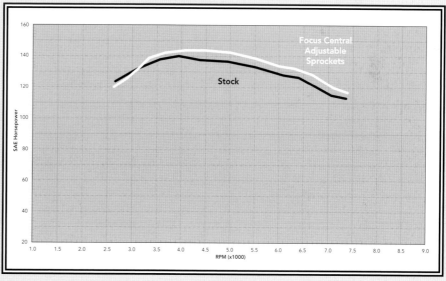

Even the mighty SVT Focus can benefit from adjustable cam timing.

If these curves are any indication, the cam timing was not optimized for maximum power from the factory.

trickery, but additional power is available by altering the exhaust cam timing via an adjustable cam sprocket. To determine the effect of installing an adjustable cam sprocket on the exhaust cam of the SVT motor, we subjected one to the dyno. Equipped with the stock (non-adjustable) cam sprocket, the mildly modified SVT motor produced peaks of 155 horsepower and 139 ft-lbs of torque. After installing and adjusting the exhaust cam sprocket, the peak power jumped to 162 horsepower, while torque improved to 144 ft-lbs. Note that the power gains were consistent from 3,000 rpm to 7,000 rpm, with just a minor dip below 3,000 rpm. Though the peak torque only increased by 5 ft-lbs, the torque gains were consistent, something that will improve acceleration much more than an elevated peak number.

WE HAVE IGNITION

CHIPS, IGNITIONS, PLUGS, & PULLEYS

Though not considered one of the Big Three, tuning is a critical element to any performance motor. Without proper tuning, all the trick ported heads, wild cam timing, and turbochargers in the world would be utterly useless. In fact, they would be as much a hindrance as a help, as adding components to provide additional airflow without the pre-scribed amount of fuel (and timing) can be a recipe for disaster. Suppose you install a trick turbo system on your Zetec or SVT Focus only to find out that the manufacturer has not supplied some form of fuel management. While some-what adaptable, the stock mass air meter and sized injectors were designed to provide adequate fuel flow for a normal-ly aspirated motor. Even if the meter was able to flow sufficient air to meet the demands of the turbocharged motor, the very best that can be expected would be a full-throttle air/fuel ratio near 13.2:1. While perfect for a normally aspirated motor, the turbo motor will melt itself down in short order with such a lean mixture.

There are a few ways to trick the factory sensors into supplying addition-al fuel under boost (from a turbo or supercharger), but the best method is to run sufficiently sized injectors along with either a recalibrated mass air meter or (even better) a reprogrammed com-puter chip. We have had much success running a set of 36-pound (RC Engi-neering) injectors and recalibrated ProM meter on turbo and supercharged Zetec motors, but the air/fuel curve is not ide-al at all boost levels. The best method would be to employ a large mass air meter (like the ProM) combined with a reprogramming to optimize both the air/fuel ratio and the associated timing curve. The problem with a repro-grammed mass air meter (like the ProM used in many of the tests) is that skew-ing the meter voltage (recalibration) also affects the timing curve. Basically, the computer sees a lower voltage from the reprogrammed meter. The lower voltage indicates less airflow and potentially less load. The ignition timing is increased at

While often overlooked, the right spark plugs, wires, and ignition system can mean the difference between a successful buildup and a misfiring monstrosity.

lower engine loads. Excessive timing can result in detonation. Though successful, the recalibrated meter is not as desirable as a dedicated chip and larger injectors.

Custom (reprogrammed) computer chips are not just for turbocharched, supercharged, or wild normally aspirated combinations, they can also be beneficial to stock and mild combos as well. Don't expect miracles from a computer, as there is not 40-50 horsepower hiding in the programming. If a chip manufacturer or tuner tries to tell you this, better steer clear of them. Most of the gains offered by custom computer chips come from additional ignition timing. Like most manufacturers, Ford was pretty conservative when it comes time to select a timing curve, and understandably so. They realize that not every Focus owner is looking for maximum performance, in fact the performance enthusiasts are a small minority. Most owners simply drive their Foci as transportation, affordable transportation at that. They are the type who run the

Test 1: Although gains on a completely stock motor are minimal, the increase in power does come with no change in underhood appearance visible to the naked eye.

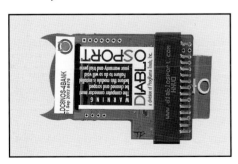

Test 1: The amount of information contained in this little chip is amazing. Some applications respond better than others to revised air/fuel and timing changes.

cheapest regular (low octane) fuel, lug the motor going up hills with the air on and generally mistreat their vehicles. It is for these owners that Ford supplied the conservative ignition curve and the reason why some additional power is available from a custom computer chip.

One problem with custom computer chips is that a new program will be necessary every time you change a component. Add different cam profiles, time for a new chip; a ported head, time for a new chip; ditto for a supercharger or even (sometimes) upping the boost pressure. One way to cure this is to install a stand-alone management system such as the unit available from Pectel. The Pectel system eliminates one of the major headaches usually associated with stand-alone systems: the hook up. Unlike a custom management system, the Pectel system was designed to be plug-n-play for the Focus. This means that the Pectel system plugs right into the factory wiring harness and utilizes most of the factory sensors. The lone exception is installing a coolant temperature sensor, something that requires only cutting a water hose and installing a T to accept the fitting. We successfully utilized the Pectel on a number of turbo combinations at elevated power levels. The Pectel was used to produce 300 hp with the F-Max kit, 365 hp with the Innovative kit, and then again on the 500-hp buildup. In addition to tuning via custom chips and the Pectel, this chapter also covers test conducted on underdrive pulleys, synthetic oil, and even nitrous oxide.

Test 1
Stock versus Diablo Chip
(Stock NA Zetec)

The first chip test took place on a mild normally aspirated motor. This test was run prior to installing the Jackson Racing supercharger. The Zetec motor was equipped with a number of minor bolt-ons, including a Borla cat-back exhaust, Focus Sport long-tube header and flex pipe, a Focus Central underdrive crank pulley and 65mm throttle body, a custom air intake system consisting of an RS Akimoto cone filter and

stock mass air meter. Initial testing indicated that the motor experienced detonation when attempting to run the Diablo chip. At the time of the test, the Focus was filled with 89-octane unleaded fuel. A single can of octane booster was necessary to raise the octane sufficiently to silence the detonation. Had the motor been run on Premium unleaded (even the 91-octane California stuff), we doubt detonation would have been present. After the octane booster, the motor ran perfectly with the new chip. Though the gains were not enormous, the Diablo chip did improve the power curve substantially down low (from 2,200 rpm to 3,700 rpm). At 2,500 rpm, the chip was responsible for a gain of 12 ft-lbs. Out near 6,000 rpm, the Diablo chip improved the peak power by 4-5 hp.

Test 2
Effect of Ignition Timing
Jackson Racing
Supercharged Zetec

The ignition timing test run with the turbo motor (see Test 3) was duplicated on a similar motor equipped with a Jackson Racing positive displacement supercharger. Oddly enough, the supercharger did not respond in the same manner as the turbo. In checking the graph, a reduction of 3 degrees of timing resulted in a loss of 4-6 horsepower. The drop in power was nowhere near as extensive as that experienced with the turbo. It is possible that the reduction in timing had a greater effect on the turbo motor because its cyclical nature. In a sense, the airflow (and therefore power output) of

Test 2: On this supercharged Zetec motor, retarding the ignition timing had a negative effect on the power output. The lesson here is that it pays to run good gas and the attending ignition timing.

Test 1: Stock vs.
Diablo Chip (Stock NA Zetec)

Engine Specifications

Block:	Stock
Crank:	Stock
Rods:	Stock
Pistons:	Stock
Head:	Stock
Valves:	Stock
Cams:	Stock
Sprockets:	Stock
Intake:	Stock
Throttle body:	65mm
Air intake:	RS Akimotot
Filter:	Cone
Maf:	Stock
Header:	Focus Sport Long Tube
Exhaust:	Borla
Injectors:	Stock
Turbo:	NA
Blower:	NA
Boost level:	NA
Management:	Stock ECU
Fuel pump:	Stock
Intercooler:	NA
Nitrous:	No

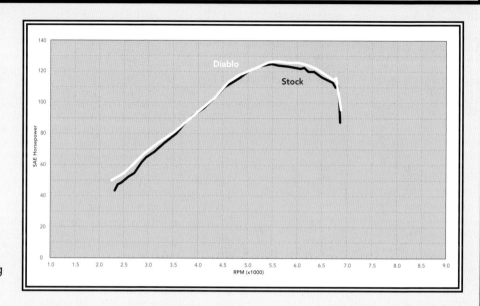

The Diablo chip improved power past 5,500 rpm, but seemed to lose power below 3,500 rpm on this application.

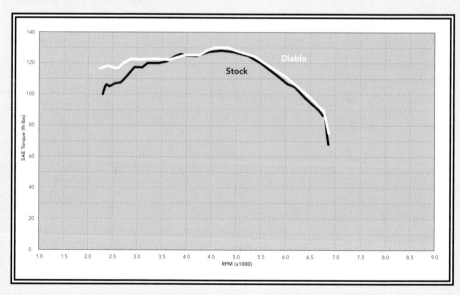

The Diablo chip was worth a few extra horses, but the gains were not what you would call significant.

If this test is any indication, don't expect big power gains from a simple chip change. The factory programming is actually pretty good.

a turbo motor is determined by the energy to the turbo. The turbo feeds on itself, as the added airflow becomes more exhaust energy, which in turn generates more airflow. Obviously the waste gate has the ultimate say in the boost and eventual power, but a reduction in the exhaust energy caused by a reduction in timing can result in less drive for the compressor. This is not the case with the blower, as the supercharger is mechanically coupled to the motor. As the motor revs, so follows the supercharger.

It should be pointed out here again that running full factory timing at these elevated boost levels can only be accomplished with a race-fuel mixture. This is especially true of the supercharger, as the inlet charge at a given boost level temperature is higher than that supplied by the turbo. When you throw in the fact that the F-Max turbo kit incorporated an air-to-air intercooler, the temps were dropped even lower. Lower charge temps mean less chance of (temperature-induced) detonation. It is also important to understand that custom chips designed to work on normally aspirated motors should almost never be run on turbo or supercharged applications. The power gains offered by custom chips usually come from increased total ignition timing. This increase in timing should never be combined with any form of forced induction, even if additional fuel is introduced. A rich mixture will not control ignition-related detonation, but a reduction in timing can affect the air/fuel ratio.

Test 2: Effect of Ignition Timing
Jackson Racing Supercharged Zetec

Engine Specifications

Block:	Stock
Crank:	Stock
Rods:	Stock
Pistons:	Stock
Head:	Focus Central ported
Valves:	Stock
Cams:	Crane 210/206
Sprockets:	Focus Central
Intake:	Jackson Racing
Throttle body:	65mm
Air intake:	Custom 3-inch
Filter:	Cone
Maf:	ProM
Header:	Focus Sport Long Tube
Exhaust:	Borla
Injectors:	36 lbs./hr.
Turbo:	NA
Blower:	Jackson Racing Eaton M62
Boost level:	10-11 psi
Management:	Stock ECU
Fuel pump:	Stock
Intercooler:	NA

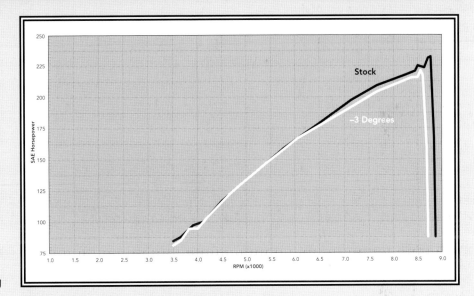

Reducing the total ignition timing across the board via the Crane HI6 resulted in a loss in power nearly across the board. This test was run to illustrate what might happen if you were forced to retard the timing to avoid detonation.

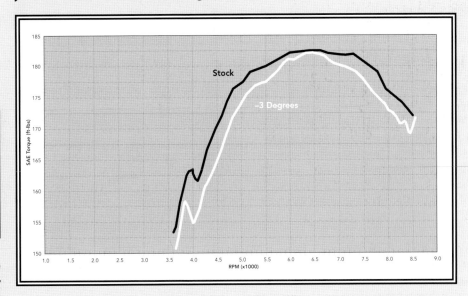

The Crane HI6 ignition amplifier is an excellent ignition upgrade, especially when adding forced induction. The increased spark energy eliminates misfiring.

The loss in torque was substantial, so running higher-octane fuel and the associated additional timing would certainly be worth power.

Test 2: Our Crane HI6 came with an ignition retard feature. All we had to do was dial out the desired amount of total ignition timing. The system can also be set up to retard under boost.

Test 3
Effect of Ignition Timing
F-Max Turbo Zetec

One of the more common methods employed to combat detonation is to retard the ignition timing. A number of ignition manufacturers offer ignition amplifiers with ignition retard capability. The ignition system used for this test was furnished by Crane Cams. The HI6 offered not only additional spark energy (necessary in boosted applications) but the ability to retard ignition timing on the Zetec motor. When it comes to detonation, engine failures are much more likely to occur with ignition-related problems than those associated with air/fuel ratio. By this we mean that your turbo or blower motor will tolerate a lean mixture much longer (though by no means indefinitely) than it will tolerate excessive ignition timing. A lean mixture will usually improve power, and the motor will likely tolerate a single dyno run at air/fuel mixtures approaching 13.5-14.0:1 (especially with high-octane race fuel). But, try it with just 1-2 degrees too much timing and the motor can let go half way through the run. This is why all of the testing with both turbo and superchargers were conducted on the dyno with high-octane race fuel and a real-time air/fuel monitor. Installing a turbo and rushing out on the street and putting your foot in it (without monitoring air/fuel or timing) is a recipe for disaster.

While retarding the timing is effective at eliminating detonation, there is a price to pay in terms of power. The ide-

al situation (for a race motor) is to run as much timing as the motor will tolerate without experiencing detonation. For a street motor, you are better off leaving the 8-10 horsepower on the table and opting for the safety of the conservative timing curve. This test was run to illustrate the effect of a reduction in timing. The Crane HI6 was employed to reduce the total timing by 4 degrees throughout the rev range. The HI6 was not configured to remove timing based on boost, but that option is available. The turbo motor was run first with full (factory) timing at 10 psi (with 100-octane fuel). The motor produced 229 horsepower at the wheels. Twisting the control knob on the Crane HI6 reduced the total timing by 4 degrees. The peak power dropped to 220 hp, but the curve was

Test 3: Once again the Crane HI6 was called into action on the Zetec motor.

Test 3: On the dyno, the loss of ignition timing (4 degrees) once again reduced the overall power curve.

Test 4: Replacing the stock damper with an underdrive pulley can free up some additional power thanks to a reduction in accessory speed.

Test 4: The stock Zetec crank pulley was both heavier and smaller in diameter than the Focus Central version.

down everywhere. Oddly enough, the turbo response improved with the timing reduction, but this was probably due to the heat induced by the first run rather than the timing. Obviously, the motor responded to the additional timing, but remember, it was done with sufficient octane to eliminate detonation.

Test 4
Stock versus Underdrive Crank
Pulley (Stock NA Zetec)

There are a number of components on your motor just waiting to steal away precious horsepower. We are not talking about internal friction, though that does indeed cost power. Rather we are talking about the parasitic losses associated with driving the various accessories. Modern vehicles (such as your Ford Focus) are equipped with a full array of comfort and convenience features. While we all enjoy cool air in the hot summer months, a feather-touch steering system to allow us to keep at least one hand free for the all-important cell-phone use, and all manner of electrically operated gizmos, all of these end up costing us power. The air conditioner, power steering, and even the alternator all effectively rob power from the motor. Pulling 8-10 horsepower from a 300-hp V8 will hardly be noticed, but pulling the same amount from a 130-hp 4-cylinder is a significant percentage of the total output. While not many Focus owners are eager to ditch the A/C, power steering, and alternator in a quest for optimum performance, there is a way to decrease the power absorbed by all of these components. Enter the underdrive crank pulley.

Underdrive pulleys are nothing new to the industry. In fact, the all of the big-three (as well as most import) auto manufacturers have experimented with

Test 3: Effect of Ignition Timing
F-Max Turbo Zetec

Engine Specifications

Block:	Stock
Crank:	Stock
Rods:	Stock
Pistons:	Stock
Head:	Focus Central ported
Valves:	Stock
Cams:	Crane 210/206
Sprockets:	Focus Central
Intake:	Stock
Throttle body:	Stock
Air intake:	F-Max 2.5-inch
Filter:	Cone
Maf:	ProM
Header:	F-Max Turbo manifold
Exhaust:	Borla
Injectors:	36 lbs./hr.
Turbo:	Turbonetics/F-Max T3/T4 Hybrid
Blower:	NA
Boost level:	10-11 psi
Management:	Stock ECU
Fuel pump:	Stock
Intercooler:	F-Max
Nitrous:	No

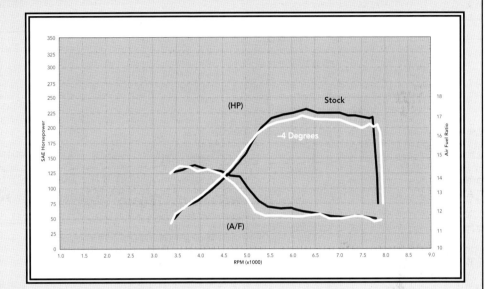

Oddly enough, a reduction in timing improved the turbo response, but reduced the overall power production.

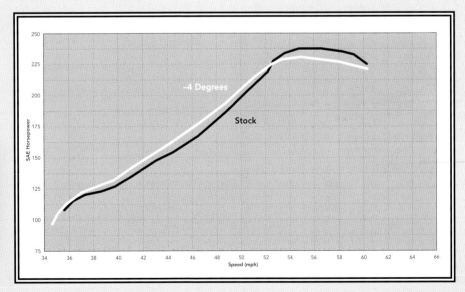

We also ran ignition timing tests on this F-Max turbo motor.

Just as with the supercharged motor, a reduction in ignition timing resulted in a dramatic drop in power.

Test 4: Stock vs. Underdrive Crank Pulley (Stock NA Zetec)

Engine Specifications

Block:	Stock
Crank:	Stock
Rods:	Stock
Pistons:	Stock
Head:	Stock
Valves:	Stock
Cams:	Stock
Sprockets:	Stock
Intake:	Stock
Throttle body:	65mm
Air intake:	RS Akimoto
Filter:	Cone
Maf:	Stock
Header:	JBA Shorty
Exhaust:	Borla
Injectors:	Stock
Turbo:	NA
Blower:	NA
Boost level:	NA
Management:	Stock ECU
Fuel pump: s	Stock
Intercooler:	NA
Nitrous:	No

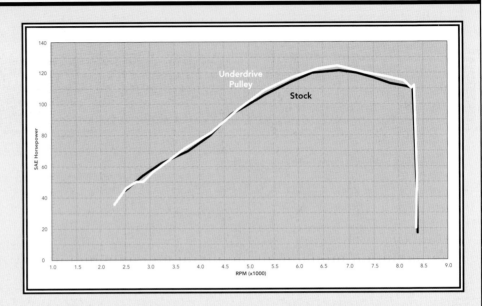

Though not huge by any means, a few horsepower here and a few there start adding up. The underdrive pulley improved the power output by 2-3 horsepower.

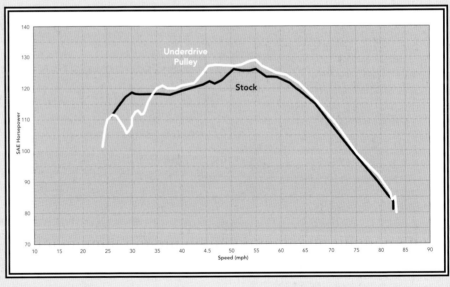

Installed on our test motor, the underdrive pulley was worth a couple of extra horses.

The greatest torque gain was 3 ft-lbs, as the power improvements increased with engine speed.

revised pulley ratios. In some cases, the revisions were to increase or decrease the speed of the water pump to control cavitations or to increase the life of accessory bearings, but the aftermarket recognized the additional power available from slowing the speed of the accessories relative to the engine. Reducing the speed of the accessories effectively increases the power available to accelerate your car. One way to decrease the speed of the accessories is to reduce the size of the crank pulley. A number of manufacturers offer underdrive pulleys (including systems designed to operate on the individual components) but altering the size of the crank pulley affects all of the accessories without resorting to individual accessory pulleys. As is illustrated by the dyno runs, replacing the heavy steel damper with a light-weight (and small–diameter) aluminum pulley resulted in a gain in power. The power gains were not huge, but note that they were present throughout the tested rev range and that they seemed to increase with engine speed. A little here and a little there—it all adds up.

**Test 5
Zex Nitrous Oxide
(Modified NA Zetec)**

One of the most affordable and effective forms of performance has to be nitrous oxide. Nitrous oxide works by delivering additional oxygen to the motor that it would not otherwise be able to ingest of its own accord. Unlike supercharging or turbocharging, which delivers additional airflow and the attending oxygen molecules that produce horsepower, nitrous oxide delivers the addi-

Test 5: Zex Nitrous Oxide
(Modified NA Zetec)

Engine Specifications

Block:	Stock
Crank:	Stock
Rods:	Stock
Pistons:	Stock
Head:	Stock
Valves:	Stock
Cams:	Crane Stage 2
Sprockets:	AEM
Intake:	Stock
Throttle body:	Stock
Air intake:	AEM
Filter:	AEM cone
Maf:	AEM
Header:	Focus Sport
Exhaust:	Focus Sport
Injectors:	Stock
Turbo:	NA
Blower:	NA
Boost level:	NA
Management:	Stock ECU
Fuel pump:	Stock
Intercooler:	NA
Nitrous:	ZEX
Jets:	50 hp

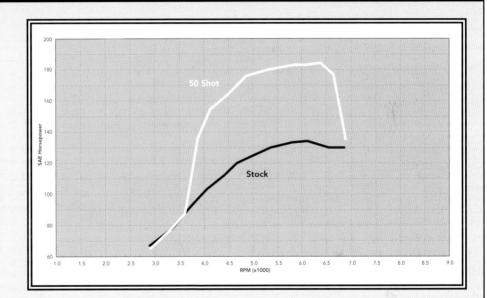

Nitrous provides serious power gains, even running a relatively small 50-hp shot. The gains offered by the nitrous were consistent as long as the system was engaged.

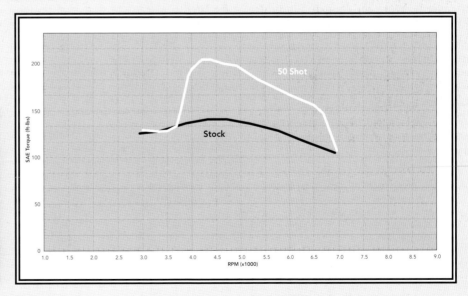

Adding 50 horsepower across the board means big torque gain below 5,250 rpm. The 50-hp shot increased the torque output by as much as 66 ft-lbs

The test mule was equipped with a mildly modified Zetec motor.

Test 5: The NX kit was adjustable from 35-75 horsepower, but we elected to run the 50-hp jetting. The kit supplied 50 hp as promised and even more torque.

Test 5: The NX system joined the fuel and nitrous together in a single fogger nozzle.

tional oxygen molecules without the extra airflow. The free oxygen molecule from this form of chemical supercharging are released when the compound is heated to approximately 572 degrees Fahrenheit. The combustion heat causes the compound to break down into its component parts, nitrogen and oxygen. In addition to the extra oxygen supplied to support (unlike depicted in the movies, nitrous oxide is not flammable) combustion, the released nitrogen actually acts as buffer, or anti-detonate, to allow a dramatic increase in power while maintaining a given detonation threshold. As a side benefit, the liquid nitrogen turns to a gas (boils) at a chilly –172 degrees, thus greatly reducing the incoming air temperature. The drop in air temps helps to further increase power by increasing the density.

While the scientific explanation of nitrous oxide is impressive, the actual results are even more so. On a modified 2.0L Zetec motor, the Zex nitrous sys-

tem increased the power output by the promised 50 horsepower. Unlike similar gains offered by conventional modifications (intake, head porting, and cams), the gains offered by nitrous oxide are present as soon as the system is activated. Important note: do not activate the nitrous oxide too early, or a backfire may occur. We activated our system at approximately 3,600 rpm and kept the system engaged until 6,600 rpm. Note that the Zex system offered a solid 50 horsepower gain from 3,750 rpm to 6,500 rpm. The 50-hp gain in power resulted in a jump in torque of 66 ft-lbs at 4,000 rpm. Chances are that a similar gain in power would easily cost you two or three times as much as the nitrous, and it is possible to go well beyond the 50-hp gain tested here, just make sure the fuel pump and injectors are up to the task of supplying the fuel necessary to safely produce the power.

Test 6
Pectel Engine Management System (Innovative Turbo Zetec)

The first thing any Focus owner notices about the accompanying graph is the exceptional power output. True enough, 518 wheel horsepower is impressive, but the real key to the power output is the line down near the bottom of the page. The line in question represents the air/fuel curve for the turbo motor during the dyno run. Note that the curve was table-top smooth in the critical area from 5,500 rpm to 7,600 rpm. The air-fuel curve was purposely richened up prior to that point, but the

curve could effectively be any shape desired thanks to the Pectel stand-alone management system and the tuning of Nathan Takuson.

The major problems associated with stand-alone fuel management systems are the need for non-factory sensors and injectors and the hassle of programming some form of base map just to get things started. The Pectel eliminates both of these problems; the first by plugging directly into the factory harness and employing the factory sensors, and the second by providing customers with base Zetec maps. In fact, since the Pectel was designed for the Zetec motor (it can also be applied to a great many other applications), the testing has produced different programs for a wide variety of Zetec engine configurations. The chances are pretty good that experts at Pectel can get even the wildest Zetec configurations up, running, and ready to tune in no time at all. The curve produced for the 518-hp turbo was perfect and took very little actual tuning. That the revised fuel system included a return-style fuel pump, 72-pound injectors, and an Aeromotive fuel pump was a testament to the flexibility of the system. Without the Pectel management system, the 500-hp turbo project would have been nothing but an exercise in frustration.

Test 7
Redline Synthetic Oil (Stock Zetec)

Like the underdrive crank pulley, synthetic lubricants don't improve the power output of your motor in the same

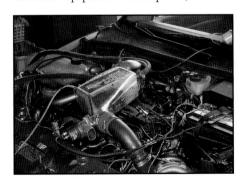

Test 6: The Pectel engine management system was put to the test on this wild turbo combination.

Test 6: The Pectel management system was designed specifically for the 2.0L Zetec motor.

Test 6: Pectel Engine Management System
(Innovative Turbo Zetec)

Engine Specifications

Block:	Stock
Crank:	Stock
Rods:	Crower
Pistons:	Sean Hyland/JE
Head:	Focus Central (Extensively ported)
Valves:	1mm oversize
Cams:	Custom Crower
Sprockets:	Focus Central
Intake:	Ford Racing
Throttle body:	65mm
Air intake:	4-inch Custom
Filter:	4x12-inch K&N
Maf:	None
Header:	Innovative Tubular
Exhaust:	Borla
Injectors:	72 lbs./hr.
Turbo:	Innovative GT66
Blower:	NA
Boost level:	29 psi
Management:	Pectel

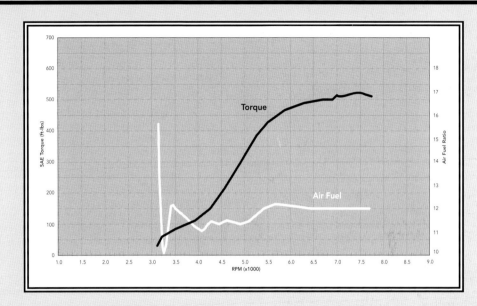

The buildup of this motor is covered in detail in chapter 8, but check out the smooth air/fuel curve produced by the Pectel engine management system. With some additional dyno time, the air/fuel curve could be any shape desired.

Fuel pump:	Aeromotive with custom return fuel system (Kenne Bell Boost-a-Pump)	Intercooler:	Vortech air-to-water Aftercooler
		Nitrous:	No

Test 6: Installation of the Pectel was quite easy, and the results were very impressive.

way as new cams or a ported intake, but rather, they release some of the power already present. Airflow improvements such as a 65mm throttle body, ported head, or free-flowing exhaust system help the motor process more air. Synthetic lubricants, like the Redline Synthetic Oil tested here, reduce the internal friction (metal on metal) that is inherent in any internal combustion engine. It is the oil's job to provide a thin layer of protection between bearings and metal reciprocating component surfaces. The better the lubricating properties (the more slippery it is), the less the friction between the two components. Less friction means the motor is easier to turn. Easy to turn means less power will be required, so the power available can be used to accelerate the vehicle and not be lost as heat buildup. Synthetic lubricants have been proven time and time again, and the Redline Synthetic Oil tested here is one of the very best lubricants available.

Though a pan full of synthetic oil will no doubt be worth additional horsepower, the real benefit comes from the ability to withstand the additional heat associated with racing, the ability to absorb additional contaminants and the longer life. Our dyno testing illustrated gains of 2-3 horsepower at the wheels, but more was available had we elected to change the tranny fluid as well. Think synthetic oil is all hype? I once ran a motor in an SCCA World Challenge race with oil temperature exceeding 350 degrees (a bearing tolerance issue). After tearing down the motor, the bearings were found to be in perfect condition and there was no wear in any of the cylinders. We credit the synthetic oil for not only saving the motor, but allowing it to run at 350 degrees in the first place. Redline makes a full range of synthetic lubricants, including high-quality power steering fluid, transmission oil, and rearend or differential lubricants. I have used Redline products in a number of my personal race cars, including high-RPM endurance motors, land-speed record setting Bon-

Test 7: Redline Synthetic Oil (Stock Zetec)

Engine Specifications

Block:	Stock
Crank:	Stock
Rods:	Stock
Pistons:	Stock
Head:	Stock
Valves:	Stock
Cams:	Stock
Sprockets:	Stock
Intake:	Stock
Throttle body:	65mm
Air intake:	RS Akimoto
Filter:	Cone
Maf:	Stock
Header:	JBA Shorty
Exhaust:	Borla
Injectors:	Stock
Turbo:	NA
Blower:	NA
Boost level:	NA
Management:	Stock ECU
Fuel pump:	Stock
Intercooler:	NA
Nitrous:	No

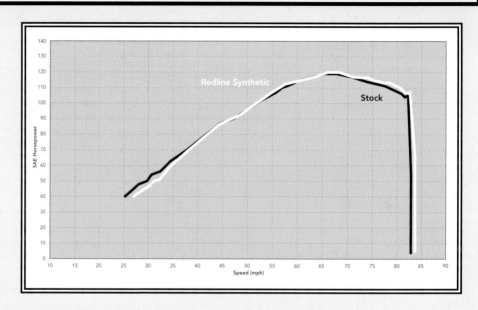

Synthetic oil is an excellent idea for any performance motor. An oil change alone can be worth 2-3 horsepower in addition to providing better lubrication and a longer interval between changes.

neville motors, and even my daily drivers (500-hp Focus, 600-hp Civic, and 800-hp Mustang). Synthetic lubricants cost more than conventional lubricants, but isn't your performance motor worth a few extra bucks?

Test 7: After dyno testing the motor with conventional oil, we filled the pan with Redline synthetic oil. The improved lubrication increased the power output by a couple of horsepower, but the real reason to use synthetic oil is for improved engine life.

Test 8
Effect of Timing
Wild Innovative Turbo Zetec)

After getting the 500-hp turbo motor up and running, it was used to run a number of tests for this book. During one of the many dyno sessions, we wanted to see what effect a few additional degrees of ignition timing would have on the power curve. It is important to note that adding ignition timing on to a motor producing 29 psi is serious business. The Pectel engine management system was initially configured to provide just 21 degrees of total timing advance across the board. Our turbo motor was fed a strict diet of Union 76 118-octane race fuel and the elevated charge temperatures were kept in line using ice water in our air-to-water intercooler system. Do not attempt to increase ignition timing on a turbo (or supercharged) motor without knowing

exactly how close the motor is to detonation. We felt comfortable adding the necessary 3 degrees given our relatively

Test 8: Big boost and increased timing don't usually go together, but our turbo motor was designed to take the abuse.

Test 8: Effect of Timing
(Wild Innovative Turbo Zetec)

Engine Specifications

Block:	Stock
Crank:	Stock
Rods:	Crower
Pistons:	Sean Hyland/JE
Head:	Focus Central (Extensively ported)
Valves:	1mm oversize
Cams:	Custom Crower
Sprockets:	Focus Central
Intake:	Ford Racing
Throttle body:	65mm
Air intake:	4-inch Custom
Filter:	4x12-inch K&N
Maf:	None
Header:	Innovative Tubular
Exhaust:	Borla
Injectors:	72 lbs./hr.
Turbo:	Innovative GT66
Blower:	NA
Boost level:	29 psi
Management:	Pectel
Fuel pump:	Aeromotive with custom return fuel system (Kenne Bell Boost-a-Pump)
Intercooler:	Vortech air-to-water Aftercooler
Nitrous:	No

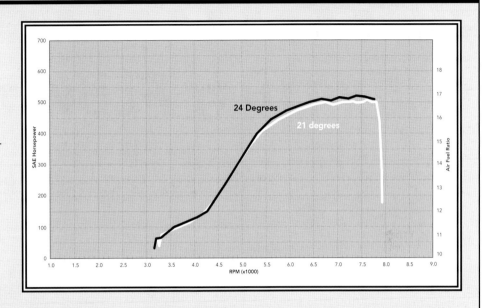

When running our big turbo motor, we experimented with additional timing. The motor was run with 118-octane fuel, a perfect air/fuel curve and an air-to-water intercooler running ice water to reduce the charge temperature. Increasing the timing by 3 degrees improved the power output by as much as 20 horsepower.

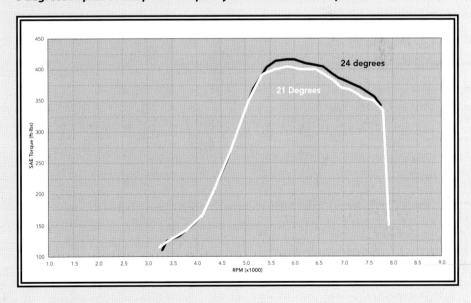

The additional timing made itself known at 5,500 rpm and improved the power output all the way to 7,700 rpm.

conservative original curve, the octane of the fuel, and the cool charge temperature. Check out the power gain offered by the increase of 3 degrees of timing (from 21 degrees to 24 degrees). If is interesting to note that the boost actually dropped ever so slightly between the first (with less timing) and the second run (with more timing). The drop was very minimal, less than 1/2 pound, but it does show that the timing was worth additional power despite the slight boost drop. Note also that the gains occurred as low as 5400 rpm, indicating that the motor was ready for the additional timing.

EXHAUST FLOW TO GO

HEADERS & CAT-BACK

The exhaust system comprises the exhaust manifold or header, the muffler, and the remainder of the exhaust tubing used to connect the exhaust manifold to the muffler and the muffler to the exhaust tip(s). Potentially sandwiched in the system are the catalytic converter, a resonator, and a flex pipe used to allow movement of the motor relative to the exhaust system. Both the Zetec and SVT Focus use a tubular header in place of the typical cast-iron exhaust manifold, although the header used on the SVT is more of the traditional long-tube design. The header used on the Zetec motor features much shorter primary tubing compared to the SVT. The header used on the Zetec looks to be designed primarily for packaging, while the SVT engineers were definitely after additional performance. One of the current trends with regards to exhaust systems is to position the catalytic converter as close as possible to the exhaust port. This aids in getting the converter up to temperature as quick as possible to reduce emissions upon initial start up.

To a minor extent, headers are much like intake manifolds, in that they act to tune the power curve. A properly designed header helps to scavenge the exhaust from an adjacent cylinder in the firing order. This is accomplished when the exhaust pulse from one primary tube is merged with another tube. The merge

For maximum power production, all of the air that finds it way into the motor must also be allowed to exit. Aiding the exhaust flow is the header and exhaust system.

causes a partial vacuum to occur in the adjacent tube. This vacuum helps pull (scavenge) the exhaust pulse that is about to occur in that cylinder. This scavenging improves the exhaust flow, but does so only at specific engine speeds. The effective engine speed is dictated by the length of the primary tubing used on the header. Longer primary length improves low-speed power production, while shorter primary lengths improve top-end horsepower. Naturally, the tubing diameter also plays a part, as does the collector diameter and length. The shorty header used on the standard Zetec motor offers very little in the way of scavenging, as the runners are all quite short and merge into a common collector. Again, this was done to provide immediate exhaust energy to the catalytic converter. Juggling header diameter and primary length can yield impressive gains in power, although the testing necessary to produce the ideal header would likely be substantial.

The discussion on the effect of header design should indicate that there is no one ideal header design for every application. Obviously the shorty header used on the stock Zetec motor is not "ideal" for that application. Ford was not looking for optimum performance when they designed that particular exhaust component. Like the other sub systems used on the Focus, cost, emissions, and noise were all major considerations. The same goes for aftermarket headers, as none of the headers tested for this book could be considered the absolute best. If there was one "ideal" header for every conceivable application, all the manufacturers would be making that design. The reality is that a four-into-one design has its strengths, as does a Tri-Y. The same can be said for large and small tube primaries, step headers, and even stock exhaust manifolds. Things really get confusing when you alter even one component on your Focus motor. Add a cam, intake, or ported head and the exhaust needs change. Even on a given combination, it is possible to trade top-end power for mid-range torque and vice versa. The question is really one of intended application, rather than finding the "ideal" design.

Test 1: Borla provided a stainless steel exhaust system for our 2001 test mule.

Test 1
Stock versus Borla Cat-Back Exhaust (Mild NA Zetec)

Along with the air intake system, one of the first performance components likely to be installed on a Zetec motor is a performance cat-back exhaust system. Again like the air intake system, maximum performance was not the major design criteria when building the exhaust for the Focus. Other considerations included cost, durability, and noise. Knowing that compromises were inherent in the stock design, Borla (along with a number of other manufacturers) went to work building their own system to improve the exhaust flow and a more authoritative exhaust note. Borla then combined the added flow and exhaust note with stainless steel construction to

ensure their customers were able to take full advantage of the added power for the life of their cars.

The 2001 Zetec Focus was only equipped with minor modifications. This is important, as the greater the

Test 2: Installed on the Zetec motor, the JBA header improved the power output in the low and mid range, but (oddly enough) offered no additional peak power.

Test 1: On the dyno, the Borla exhaust increased the power output and offered a much improved sound quality.

Test 2: The JBA shorty header offered improved exhaust flow thanks to larger diameter tubing and better merge points.

Test 1: Stock vs. Borla Cat-Back Exhaust (Mild NA Zetec)

Engine Specifications

Block:	Stock
Crank:	Stock
Rods:	Stock
Pistons:	Stock
Head:	Stock
Valves:	Stock
Cams:	Stock
Sprockets:	Stock
Intake:	Stock
Throttle body:	65mm
Air intake:	AEM
Filter:	AEM cone
Maf:	AEM
Header:	Stock
Exhaust:	Stock vs Borla
Injectors:	Stock
Turbo:	NA
Blower:	NA
Boost level:	NA
Management:	Stock ECU
Fuel pump:	Stock
Intercooler:	NA
Nitrous:	No

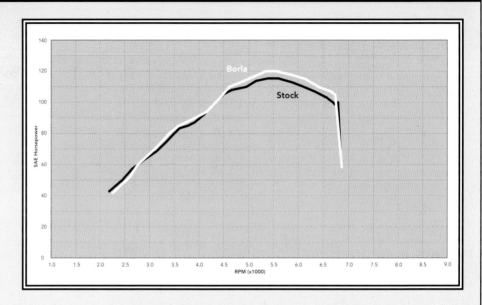

The Borla stainless cat-back exhaust system was worth some additional power over the stock exhaust, even on this mild combination.

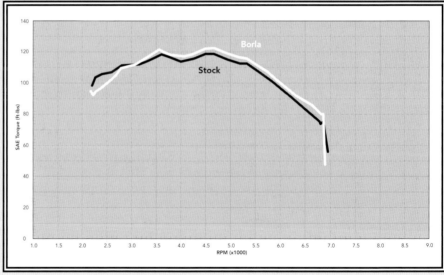

The Borla was worth 3-5 ft-lbs of torque throughout the rev range.

The factory Ford exhaust system was both restrictive and too quiet.

modifications (and power output), the greater the power gains offered by an aftermarket exhaust. Even given the mild combination, the Borla exhaust improved the power output of the Zetec motor by over 6 horsepower, with gains starting as low as 3000 rpm and continuing until red line.

Test 2
Stock versus JBA Shorty Header (Mild NA Zetec)

The results of this test were somewhat of a surprise, so much so that the test was rerun to verify the results. Unlike a number of production pieces,

the stock Zetec Focus exhaust manifold is not a casting. Instead, the Focus relies on what can be described as a tubular header, though header might be stretching things a bit given the convoluted nature of the design. The stock exhaust manifold exits the head, makes a 90-degree turn upward followed by another 90-degree turn inward and then a third 90-degree turn downward, where the four exhaust tubes merge into a 3-bolt triangular flange used to attach the catalytic converter. Naturally, the tubing diameter, effective length, and merge points were done more for packaging rather than optimum exhaust scavenging and power production. One of the first companies on the scene with a replacement header was JBA. Their tubular header featured larger tubing, smoother bends, and a custom merge all designed to improve exhaust flow. Testing with the JBA shorty header produced some

Test 2: Stock vs. JBA Shorty Header (Mild NA Zetec)

Engine Specifications

Block:	Stock
Crank:	Stock
Rods:	Stock
Pistons:	Stock
Head:	Stock
Valves:	Stock
Cams:	Stock
Sprockets:	Stock
Intake:	Stock
Throttle body:	65mm
Air intake:	AEM
Filter:	AEM cone
Maf:	AEM
Header:	Stock
Exhaust:	Borla
Injectors:	Stock
Turbo:	NA
Blower:	NA
Boost level:	NA
Management:	Stock ECU
Fuel pump:	Stock
Intercooler:	NA
Nitrous:	No

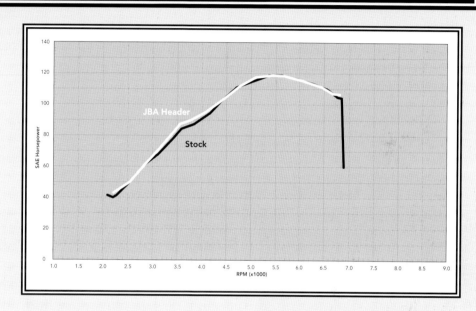

The results of this test were somewhat surprising, as we expected the power gains offered by the JBA header to be near the top of the rev range (typical of airflow improvements). The JBA header improved power from 2,800 rpm to 5,200 rpm, but there was little change in peak power.

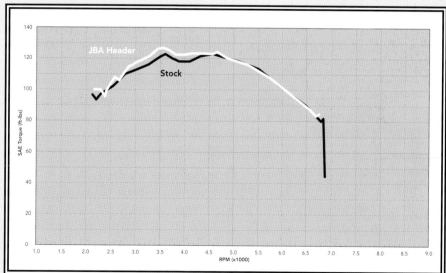

Though stainless steel and tubular, the stock exhaust manifold left something to be desired in terms of flow.

The tubular JBA (shorty) header was worth 3-5 ft-lbs of torque over the stock exhaust manifold.

unusual results. Though we were not expecting huge gains given the similarity to the stock design, we expected the JBA header to improve power with engine speed. What happened was the opposite, as the JBA header posted power gains at low RPM, but did not show improvements in power beyond 5000 rpm. To verify the results, we removed the JBA header and reran the test. The results were identical.

Test 3
JBA versus Focus Sport Long- Tube Header & Off Road Pipe (Mild NA Zetec)

After running and rerunning the test on the JBA shorty header, we did not know what to expect before installing the Focus Sport long-tube header and off-road pipe. Long-tube headers work by pairing adjacent cylinders in the firing

Test 3: After running the JBA shorty header, we were curious about the power potential of a dedicated long-tube header.

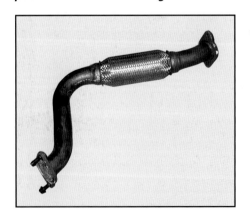

Test 3: Focus Sport also supplied a 3-inch flex pipe, though testing showed that most of the gains came from the long-tube header.

order. The idea behind pairing cylinders is that as the exhaust rushes out of one tube, it helps create a vacuum in the adjacent tube. This vacuum helps pull the exhaust out of the adjacent. This scavenging effect helps improve the exhaust flow and therefore the power output of the motor. Just like the intake manifold, the length of the header tubing determines when the scavenging is most effective. Tune the scavenging effect with the runner length in the intake and you have the makings of a powerful combination. Now provide cam timing to maximize power production in the chosen RPM range where the intake tuning and exhaust scavenging are most effective and you have a serious power producer. Naturally, arriving at the ideal combination takes a great deal of testing. Just imagine all the possible combinations that could be tested using different intake lengths, different exhaust lengths, and changes in cam lift and duration. It boggles the mind.

One of the problems with shorty headers is that they provide very little scavenging. The majority of the power gains offered by shorty headers come from increasing the exhaust flow, basically making them less restrictive than their stock counterparts. Though additional flow can be beneficial, the scavenging or pulse tuning is every bit as important when making power. This test combined exhaust flow improvements with the scavenging effect offered by the long-tube header design. The mild 2.0L Zetec was run first with the JBA shorty header and then again with the Focus Sport long-tube header. The long-tube header also required removal of the catalytic converter, something run with the JBA shorty header. Removing the JBA header and installing the long-tube header resulted in a gain of 4 peak horsepower. The gains were as high as 5-6 horsepower elsewhere in the curve, with majority of the power gains occurring after 4000 rpm. Just as with the Borla cat-back exhaust, we suspect that the power gains offered by the long-tube header and off-road pipe would have been even greater had we elected to test them on a slightly wilder engine configuration.

Test 4
Stock versus Off-Road Pipe (Turbocharged Zetec)

One of the common misconceptions, at least one expressed daily on the internet, is that catalytic converters rob the motor of every last ounce of horsepower. While it is true that a catalytic converter can hurt exhaust flow, they are hardly the major power culprit everyone makes them out to be. Case in point, while running this particular test, a well-meaning but obviously uninformed Focus owner happened to stop by the shop while we were in the process of installing the off-road pipe. When we explained what we were doing, he informed us that he recently installed an off-road pipe on his normally aspirated Focus and that it had to be worth an

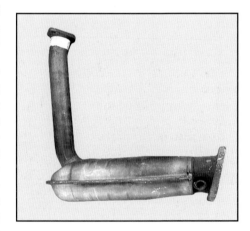

Test 4: It should not be surprising that the stock catalytic converter can restrict exhaust flow.

Test 4: On our turbo motor, the off-road pipe did not show a dramatic improvement in power. It's possible this test might be flawed by an exhaust leak before the turbo.

Test 3: JBA vs. Focus Sport Long Tube Header & Off Road Pipe (Mild NA Zetec)

Engine Specifications

Block:	Stock
Crank:	Stock
Rods:	Stock
Pistons:	Stock
Head:	Stock
Valves:	Stock
Cams:	Stock
Sprockets:	Stock
Intake:	Stock
Throttle body:	65mm
Air intake:	RS Akimoto
Filter:	RS Akimoto Cone
Maf:	Stock
Header:	JBA shorty vs. Focus Sport Long Tube
Exhaust:	Borla
Injectors:	Stock
Turbo:	NA
Blower:	NA
Boost level:	NA
Management:	Stock ECU
Fuel pump:	Stock
Intercooler:	NA
Nitrous:	No

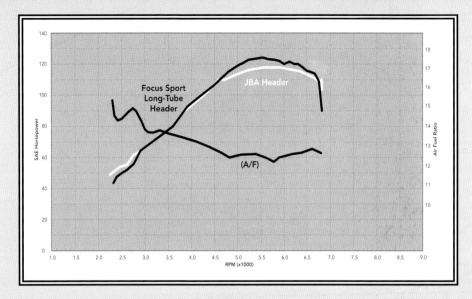

Replacing the shorty JBA header and catalytic converter with a Focus Sport long-tube header and off-road pipe resulted in a maximum gain of 8-9 horsepower.

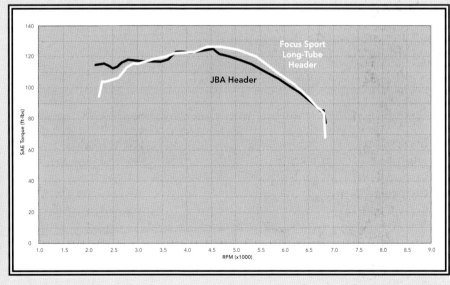

Focus Sport supplied a long-tube header for testing.

Most of the additional torque offered by the header and off-road pipe occurred after 4,500 rpm.

easy 20 horsepower. Naturally, we asked if he ran the motor on a dyno before and after the installation, and as usual, the answer was no. He was very adamant that we were going to get even more than the proverbial 20 horsepower on our turbo motor, since it was making so much more power than his all-motor combination. Such is the misconception.

Before removing the stock converter, the motor was run in turbocharged form with the F-Max turbo kit set at 7 psi. The turbo motor was run with a ProM mass air meter recalibrated for the larger 36 pound-per-hour injectors. With the stock catalytic converter in place, the turbo motor produced 188 horsepower. After removing the converter and replacing it with an off-road pipe from Focus Central, the turbo motor produced 192 horsepower, for a

Test 4: Stock vs. Off-Road Pipe (Turbocharged Zetec)

Engine Specifications

Block:	Stock
Crank:	Stock
Rods:	Stock
Pistons:	Stock
Head:	Focus Central Ported
Valves:	Stock
Cams:	Crane 210/206
Sprockets:	Focus Central
Intake:	Stock
Throttle body:	Stock
Air intake:	F-Max
Filter:	Cone
Maf:	ProM
Header:	F-Max Turbo Manifold
Exhaust:	Borla
Injectors:	36 lbs./hr.
Turbo:	F-Max
Blower:	NA
Boost level:	7 psi
Management:	Stock ECU
Fuel pump:	Stock
Intercooler:	F-Max air-to-air
Nitrous:	No

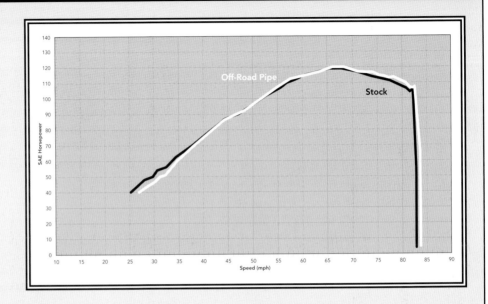

Installation of the off-road pipe on the turbo motor resulted in a drop in response to the turbo, but more peak power thanks to better exhaust flow. The results of this test seem contrary to what would be expected, a freeing up a restriction in the exhaust will usually improve turbo response. I can't help but wonder if an exhaust or intake leak was present to skew the results.

gain of 4 horsepower peak-to-peak. Where was the 20+ horsepower promised by our Focus friend? The reality is that the stock converter is not that restrictive, even at this elevated power level. We have made over 250 wheel horsepower with the stock cat and see

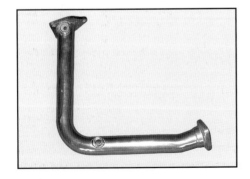

Test 4: Our testing involved replacing the stock cat with an off-road pipe.

no reason why 300 wheel horsepower isn't possible. Note from the curves that installing the off-road pipe actually reduced the response of the turbo, something we thought was odd given results of previous testing. This type of anomaly is why it is so important to include the full power curve and not just the peak numbers.

Test 5
Focus Sport Long Tube versus Focus Central Long Tube (JR Supercharged Zetec)

While testing exhaust components, we noticed a difference between the long-tube header offered by Focus Central and the header offered by Focus Sport. The Focus Central header was of the Tri-Y design, meaning that each pair

of the four primary pipes merged to form two secondary pipes. These two pipes then merged to form a single collector. The three separate merges produced three distinct Y shapes in the header—thus the Tri-Y designation. By contrast, the Focus Sport header was a

Test 5: The Focus Sport header was a 4-into-1 design that featured slightly larger primary tubing.

more conventional 4-into-1 design, where all four of the primary pipes merged at one point to produce a common collector. Exhaust theory dictates that the Tri-Y design will typically produce scavenging at different engine speeds than the conventional 4-into-1. Rather than let exhaust theory dictate what happens, we decided to put the two headers to the test on a supercharged Zetec motor. The thinking was that the supercharged motor would respond to changes in the exhaust system more readily, as the artificial induction system placed more of a demand on the exhaust system.

The test motor featured a Jackson Racing supercharger kit featuring a prototype M62 supercharger. The standard supercharger kits for the Zetec motor utilize the smaller M45 blower, while the M62 is reserved for the new SVT kit. The motor also featured mild head porting, small Crane cams, and a 65mm throttle

Test 5: Focus Sport Long Tube vs. Focus Central Long Tube (JR Supercharged Zetec)

Engine Specifications

Block:	Stock
Crank:	Stock
Rods:	Stock
Pistons:	Stock
Head:	Focus Central ported
Valves:	Stock
Cams:	Crane 210/206
Sprockets:	Focus Central
Intake:	Jackson Racing
Throttle body:	65mm
Air intake:	Custom 3-inch
Filter:	Cone
Maf:	ProM
Header:	Focus Sport Long Tube vs Focus Central Long Tube
Exhaust:	Borla
Injectors:	30 lbs./hr.
Turbo:	NA
Blower:	Jackson Racing M62
Boost level:	11 psi
Management:	Stock ECU
Fuel pump:	Stock
Intercooler:	NA
Nitrous:	No

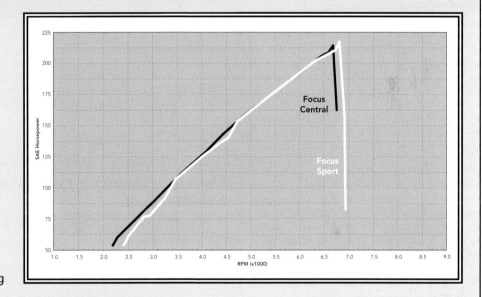

The graph indicates that the 4 into 1 header lost some low-speed power compared to the Tri-Y design.

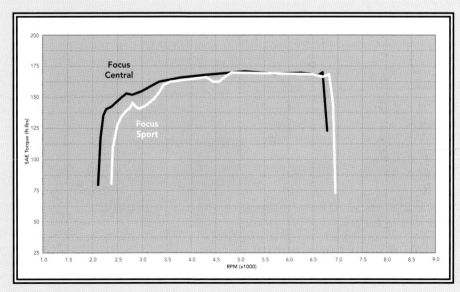

The tri-y design offered significant torque gains at 3,000 rpm.

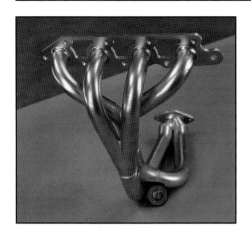

Test 5: The Focus Central long-tube header was a tri-y design that offered smaller diameter primary tubing.

body. The blower was set up to provide 10-11 psi of boost. So equipped, the motor produce 212 horsepower at 6,700 rpm with the Focus Central long tube header and off-road pipe installed. After swapping the Focus Sport 4-into-1 header, the peak power remained at 212 horsepower, but the 4-into-1 design actually lost some low-speed power from 2,500 rpm to 3,200 rpm and then again from 4,400 rpm to 4,700 rpm. From 4,700 rpm to 6,700 rpm, the two power curves were otherwise identical. Credit the exhaust scavenging of the Tri-Y design for the improvement in low-speed power. These results should by no means be considered absolute, as the

supercharged motor may well respond differently than a comparable normally aspirated motor. Remember too that not many normally aspirated street Zetec motors produced 212 wheel horsepower.

Test 6
Stock Cat versus
Off-Road Pipe versus
Focus Central Long Tube
(Stock SVT)

The SVT Focus has a number of great things going for it. The engine configuration is much improved over the Zetec version, featuring such improvements as higher compression, a dual-runner intake, and even a long-tube header right from the factory. As good as the factory stuff is, even from the experts at SVT, there is always room for improvement. Take the tubular SVT header for instance. Though tubular and a real long-tube design, there are ways to improve upon the factory SVT header. Not surprisingly, the same can be said for the stock catalytic converter. This test involved an SVT Focus equipped with the factory tubular header and catalytic converter. The first test involved removing the converter and replacing it with an off-road pipe from Focus Central. Equipped with the stock SVT header and cat, the 2.0L motor produced 141 horsepower at 7,000 rpm and 128 ft-lbs

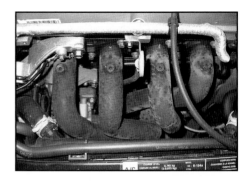

Test 6: Unlike the standard Zetec model, the SVT Focus was equipped with a long-tube header from the factory.

of torque at 3,000 & 5,000 rpm (effect of dual-runner intake). Installing the off-road pipe improved the power at 7,000 rpm to 148 horsepower, while the torque peak jumped to 132 ft-lbs at 4,000 rpm. Note from the graph that the horsepower improved from 3,000 rpm to 7,000 rpm, a sure sign that the cat was restricting exhaust flow.

Installing the Focus Central 1-3/4-inch race header resulted in another significant power gain. Though offering plenty of total exhaust flow, the SVT header was obviously not optimized to take full advantage of the scavenging effect offered by each pipe. Naturally, this scavenging effect depends on the primary length (and diameter) in relation to the engine speed. This scavenging effect is not always present, but when it is, the exhaust flow is greatly enhanced. Obviously the Focus Central race header utilized this pulse tuning to

Test 5: On our supercharged test motor, the smaller diameter Focus Central header improved low-speed power production without sacrificing any top-end power.

Test 7: The author fabricated this custom exhaust pipe to connect the turbo to the Borla cat-back. Note the header wrap used to keep heat off wiring and other engine components.

Test 6: Stock Cat vs. Off-Road Pipe vs. Focus Central Long Tube (Stock SVT)

Engine Specifications

Block:	Stock SVT
Crank:	Stock SVT
Rods:	Stock SVT
Pistons:	Stock SVT
Head:	Stock SVT
Valves:	Stock SVT
Cams:	Stock SVT
Sprockets:	Stock SVT
Intake:	Stock SVT
Throttle body:	Stock SVT
Air intake:	Stock SVT
Filter:	Stock SVT
Maf:	Stock SVT
Header:	Stock SVT vs. Focus Central Long Tube
Exhaust:	SVT
Injectors:	Stock SVT
Turbo:	NA
Blower:	NA
Boost level:	NA
Management:	Stock ECU
Fuel pump:	Stock
Intercooler:	NA
Nitrous:	No

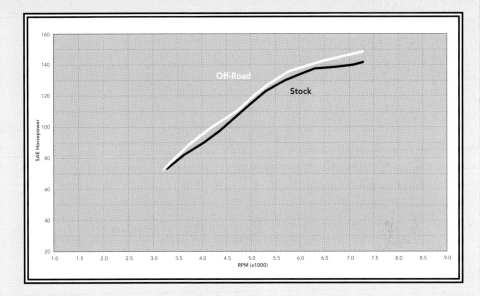

Installation of the off-road pipe on the SVT Focus resulted in a sizable power gain, from 3,400 rpm all the way to redline.

Even the mighty SVT Focus will respond to exhaust tuning.

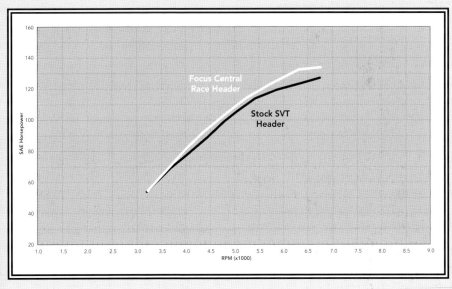

Swapping the stock SVT header for a Focus Central race header resulted in another sizable power gain.

improve the power output, as the race header improved the power output of the SVT motor by as much as 9 horsepower (at 6,500 rpm). Like the off-road pipe, the race header improved the power output nearly across the board, from 3,500 rpm to 7,000 rpm.

Test 7
Borla Cat-Back versus
No Exhaust (Turbo Zetec)

While testing the turbo motor in cChapter 7, we were curious about how restrictive the Borla cat-back exhaust was

at such an elevated power level. Clearly Borla never envisioned the exhaust system to be installed on a motor that produced more than 3 times the original output. Obviously the airflow pumped into the 350-hp turbo motor had to find its way out. The turbine flange of the

Test 7: Borla Cat-Back vs. No Exhaust (Turbo Zetec)

Engine Specifications

Block:	Stock
Crank:	Stock
Rods:	Stock
Pistons:	Stock
Head:	Focus Central Ported
Valves:	Stock
Cams:	Crane Stage 1
Sprockets:	AEM
Intake:	Focus Central Ported 2000
Throttle body:	Stock
Air intake:	Custom 3.5-inch
Filter:	K&N Cone
Maf:	None
Header:	Ken Duttweiller/Innovative Turbo
Exhaust:	Borla vs. no Exhaust
Injectors:	72 lbs./hr,
Turbo:	Innovative T04E-46
Blower:	NA
Boost level:	22 psi
Management:	Pectel Stand Alone
Fuel pump:	Stock with Kenne Bell Boost-a-Pump
Intercooler:	Vortech Aftercooler (air-to-water)
Nitrous:	No

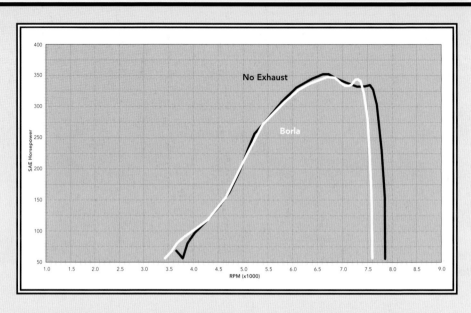

Designed for a 130-hp Zetec motor, the Borla cat-back exhaust was obviously over-engineered, as the exhaust represented very little restriction at the 350-hp level.

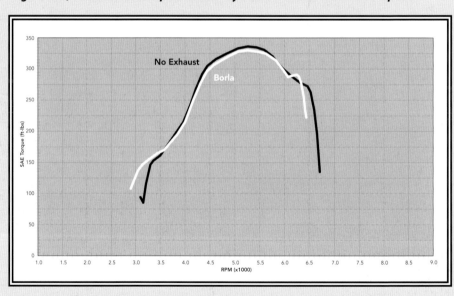

The torque difference was minimal, indicating that the Borla street exhaust offered plenty of flow, not to mention a quieter exhaust note.

T04E-46 turbo featured a 2.5-inch outlet. A mating flange (supplied by Innovative Turbo) was fabricated to allow use of a 2.5-inch exhaust to be mated to the back of the turbo. This was a custom setup and not part of any turbo kit. The 2.5-inch down pipe was then connected to the Borla cat-back exhaust. While testing the turbo motor at various boost levels, we couldn't help but wonder if the cat-back exhaust system was restricting the power output of the motor; after all, the cat-back exhaust was never designed to flow 350 hp worth of air.

Testing our exhaust restriction theory was quite simple, all we had to do was disconnect the Borla cat-back system from the down pipe. This essentially eliminated the Borla from the system and allowed the exhaust to free flow out of the 2.5-inch length of tubing.

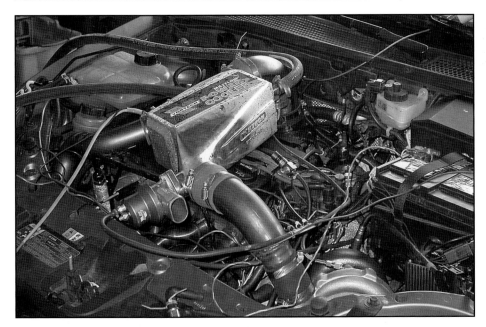

Test 8: In this second test on an off-road pipe, the stock cat proved to be somewhat restrictive on this mild, naturally aspirated Zetec.

Test 7: Running a T04E-46 turbo on the stock short block produced 350 hp through the Borla cat-back exhaust.

Equipped with the Borla, the motor (at 22 psi) produced 350 horsepower. After dropping the Borla, the peak power increased to just 353 horsepower, indicating that the Borla flowed nearly as well as no exhaust at all. Naturally the motor sounded much better, not to mention quieter with the high-quality, stainless steel Borla system. Given that it would be next to impossible to drive the turbo Focus around on a daily basis with an open exhaust (even muffled by the turbo), it is nice to know that the Borla didn't seem to offer much of a restriction, even at 3 times the intended power level.

Test 8
Stock Cat versus
Off-Road Pipe (Mild NA Zetec)

Though simple and straightforward, this test of the effectiveness of the stock catalytic converter was one of the final tests run for this book (the 500-hp

buildup being the swan song). It should come as no surprise that the catalytic converter is a hindrance to exhaust flow, and anything that can be done to remove said restriction should help in the horsepower department. As it turned out, removing the converter on this particular application was worth a great deal of power, especially as the engine speed increased. That the majority of the power gains appeared near the top of the rev range was not surprising. This is typical of restriction in airflow, both intake and exhaust. As the airflow of the motor is increased (with engine speed), restric-

Test 7: On the dyno, dropping the Borla cat-back exhaust altogether was worth only 3 peak horsepower. The Borla flowed nearly as well as having no exhaust at all.

Test 8: The mild motor picked up 11-12 horsepower, indicating that the stock cat was restricting exhaust flow.

tions become more pronounced, thus removing the restrictions produces greater power gains. Check out the gains experienced by installing a prototype air intake system on a Jackson Racing supercharged SVT in Chapter 6 to see a textbook example an inlet restriction that increases with engine speed. Removing the catalytic converter did very little to the power curve until the tach swung past 4,500 rpm. The gains increased, especially past 6,000 rpm, where the off-road pipe was worth 11-12 horsepower. It is interesting to note that the power gains offered by the off-road were much greater on this mild Zetec application than the more powerful turbo motor tested elsewhere in this chapter.

Test 8: Stock Cat vs. Off-Road Pipe (Mild NA Zetec)

Engine Specifications

Block:	Stock
Crank:	Stock
Rods:	Stock
Pistons:	Stock
Head:	Stock
Valves:	Stock
Cams:	Stock
Sprockets:	AEM
Intake:	Focus Central Modified
Throttle body:	65mm
Air intake:	Steeda
Filter:	Steeda
Maf:	ProM
Header:	JBA Shorty
Exhaust:	Custom 2.5-inch
Injectors:	Stock
Turbo:	NA
Blower:	NA
Boost level:	NA
Management:	Stock ECU
Fuel pump:	Stock
Intercooler:	NA
Nitrous:	No

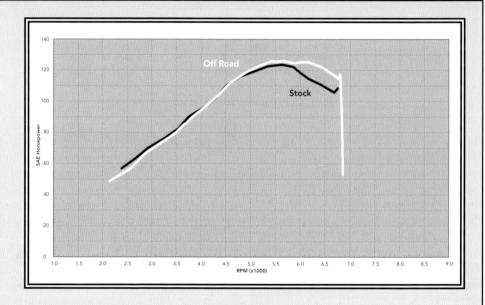

The results of this test indicate that our previous test on the off-road pipe may have been flawed. The off-road pipe did improve power over the stock cat on this mild Zetec application, though most of the power gains occurred past 5,700 rpm.

The off-road pipe replaced the stock cat to improve exhaust flow.

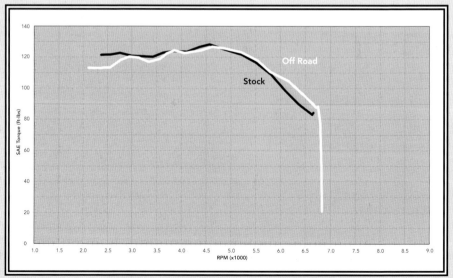

The difference in power was minimal until high RPM, something we have come to expect of airflow (or exhaust) restriction removal.

BOOST BUILDERS

THE SCIENCE OF SUPERCHARGING

Shortly after receiving a 2001 Ford Focus ZX3 from Ford, I began to wonder if it was possible to extract V8 performance from the little Zetec motor. To that end, I set forth on a buildup that would eventually allow the ZX3 to post 1/4-mile times quicker and faster than a 2001 4.6L Mustang GT. While 13-second Foci are more common now, it was very rare to run across an honest-to-goodness 13-second Focus on the street back in 2001. After scanning the marketplace, I determined that the all-motor route was not feasible. It would take a dedicated race motor combined with a strict weight loss program to allow the Focus to knock down real 13-second time slips. Since then, Dennis from Focus Central has managed to run 12s in all-motor form, using the stock short block no less. Time and technology continue to march on. With little in the way of hardcore (all-motor) performance parts available, I turned to my old friend, forced induction. Enter the Jackson Racing supercharger.

Even before I received the 2001 ZX3 from Ford, Jackson Racing had produced a supercharger kit for the 2.0L Zetec motor. The base kit utilized the M45 Eaton supercharger to provide approximately 5 psi of boost. Adding the supercharger upped the power output of a stock Zetec from 109 hp (at the wheels) to 148 hp. The Jackson Racing supercharger kit increased the power peak by over 35%. Additional tuning, more boost and a revised inlet system upped the power level near 180 wheel horsepower using the same M45 supercharger. While slightly more power was possible by further increasing the boost pressure supplied by the M45, my goal was to equal the power output of the 4.6L V8 Mustang. Rated at 260 flywheel horsepower, the 5-speed 4.6L GT would put down 235 wheel horsepower. The 235 hp number was my goal with the supercharger Zetec motor. Obviously, the small M45 supercharger was not capable of supporting that much power, but Oscar Jackson still had a trick or two up his sleeve.

His trick involved replacing the smaller M45 supercharger with the larg-

When it comes to improving the power output of a motor, there is nothing like the immediate boost response of a Jackson Racing supercharger.

er M62 Eaton used on his more powerful Honda/Acura and SVT Focus kits. The M62 offered more than enough flow potential to reach of goal of 235 wheel horsepower. When combined with a ported head, cams and a good exhaust system, the Jackson Racing supercharged Focus easily eclipsed the 13-second mark at over 102 mph. Running 12-13 psi, the supercharged Zetec pumped out 235 wheel horsepower and 192 ft-lbs of torque. The great thing about supercharging (as opposed to turbos) is that a well-designed supercharger kit running a positive displacement supercharger (like the Eaton M45 and M62) will provide immediate boost response. There is no waiting for the turbo to spool up, just mash on the gas and you have boost. The downside of the immediate response is that the tuning must be spot on, or detonation may rear its ugly head. The Roots supercharger will also never be able to equal the power levels of the turbo, but (as of this writing) there were no emission legal turbo kits available for the Focus. The Jackson Racing kit not only provided immediate boost response, but also full emissions compliance (in 5 psi M45 form).

Just as this book was nearing completion, another manufacturer joined Jackson Racing to provide superchargers to Focus Owners. Kenne Bell, a name synonymous with blazing Buicks and street supercharging, designed and built a kit for the Focus using a twin-screw supercharger from Autorotor. Though positive displacement like the Eaton, the Autorotor features improved efficiency and airflow potential thanks to the unique twin-screw rotors. Rather than simply pump air from one side of the supercharger to another, the Autorotor was actually a true compressor (though to a lesser extent than a turbo or centrifugal supercharger). Extensive testing has shown that given identical dimensions and blower speed, the twin-screw design will always out-perform a Roots supercharger both in terms of airflow and inlet temperature. The benefit to the Focus owner can be a gain in power with a reduction in charge temperature using the Kenne Bell (Autorotor) supercharger. A number of

prototype kits existed featuring centrifugal superchargers, but no production pieces were available for testing prior to the deadline of this book. (Vortech did complete a supercharger kit for the Focus as this went to print).

Test 1
Stock Zetec versus
Jackson Racing Supercharger

One company was involved early in the performance development of the 2.0L Zetec, Jackson Racing. Once a name synonymous with racing Hondas, Jackson Racing has proven to be one of *the* sources for forced induction of not just Hondas, but a number of other cars, including the Ford Focus. The Jackson Racing supercharger kitis based on an M45 Eaton positive displacement supercharger capable of pumping out 5-6 psi. Though capable of more boost (and

Test 1: The Jackson Racing supercharger kit was an honest-to-goodness bolt-on modification that (unlike most of the mods covered in the book) has full emissions certification.

Test 1: The supercharged motor pumped out 147 wheel horsepower, up from just 109 in stock trim.

power), the emissions-legal 2.0L Zetec kit from Jackson Racing was set at 5-6 psi. The importance of the emissions legality can't be overstressed here, as it is often times quite easy to produce exceptional power using wild cam timing, nitrous oxide or even turbocharging, but doing so with full emissions compliance has proven difficult for all but a handful of tuners. Jackson Racing has found a way to greatly improve the power output of the Ford Focus without harming emissions production.

Rated at 130 flywheel horsepower in stock trim, a 2.0L Zetec Focus motor will usually produce somewhere in the neighborhood of 105hp-109hp at the wheels. We have seen motors produce only 101 wheel horsepower as well as a few that have exceeded 110 hp. In addition to the supercharger, the Jackson Racing supercharger kit included a dedicated intake manifold, alternator relocation bracket and all the necessary mounting hardware and accessories to increase the power output by a solid 40-45 horsepower. Though the peak torque increase was only 15-17 ft-lbs, the torque gains are as great as 35-40 ft-lbs higher in the rev range. It is certainly possible to build a normally aspirated Zetec motor to produce 145-150 wheel horsepower, but it would be difficult if not impossible to do it in emissions certified form. While many states have not adopted California's stringent emission standards, it is only a matter of time before the rest of the country follows suit. In time, it will become more and more difficult to "get around" annual smog checks. Lucky for us, companies like Jackson Racing have found ways to certify the extra horsepower we all crave.

Test 2
Jackson Racing Supercharger
versus Big-Boost Upgrade

While the standard Jackson Racing supercharger kit for the 2.0L Zetec can significantly improve the power output of a stock motor, there are always Focus enthusiasts wanting more. It is for these customers that Jackson Racing developed the Big-Boost upgrade kit. The upgrade kit consisted of a different

Test 1: Stock Zetec vs. Jackson Racing Supercharger

Engine Specifications

Block:	Stock
Crank:	Stock
Rods:	Stock
Pistons:	Stock
Head:	Stock
Valves:	Stock
Cams:	Stock
Sprockets:	Stock
Intake:	Jackson Racing
Throttle body:	Stock
Air intake:	Stock Air Box
Filter:	Stock
Maf:	Stock
Header:	Stock Exhaust Manifold
Exhaust:	Stock
Injectors:	Stock 19 lbs./hr.
Turbo:	NA
Blower:	Jackson Racing M45
Boost level:	5-6 psi
Management:	Stock ECU + JR Fuel Controller
Fuel pump:	Stock
Intercooler:	NA
Nitrous:	No

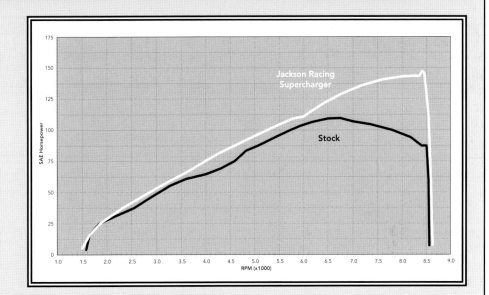

Adding the Jackson Racing supercharger increased the power peak from 109 wheel horsepower to 147 wheel horsepower. The loss of intake runner length resulted in only minimal power gains up to 3000 rpm, despite the presence of boost pressure below this point.

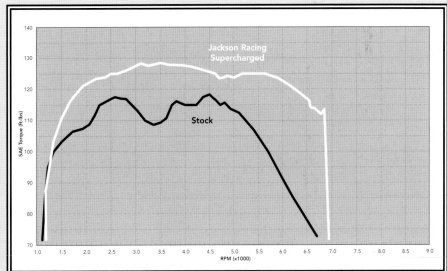

The short runners on the Jackson Racing supercharger kit flattened and extended the torque curve. The supercharged motor produced near 125 ft-lbs of torque from 2,500 rpm all the way to 6,500 rpm.

The stock 130-hp 2.0L Zetec motor can definitely use a boost in power.

supercharger pulley to increase the boost pressure by 2 psi, a larger 65mm throttle body and a revised intake system including a mass air meter and 30-pound injectors. Naturally, a smaller blower pulley that increased the boost pressure by 2 psi makes a significant difference in power, but the increase in boost is only a part of the equation. Knowing (through extensive testing) that supercharged motors are extremely sensitive to inlet restrictions, Jackson

Racing designed an intake system to minimize any restrictions. The result was a system consisting of a cone filter, 3-inch tubing, and a provision for the mass air meter electronics. The inlet and boost changes were augmented by swapping in larger fuel injectors. The stock 19 lbs./hr. injectors were not able to support the power level developed by the upgrade modifications. On the dyno, the upgrade elevated the peak power to 181 horsepower, while torque jumped from 131 ft-lbs to 155 ft-lbs. Naturally the gains were consistent throughout the rev range.

Test 2: Jackson Racing Supercharger vs. Big-Boost Upgrade

Engine Specifications

Block:	Stock
Crank:	Stock
Rods:	Stock
Pistons:	Stock
Head:	Stock
Valves:	Stock
Cams:	Stock
Sprockets:	Stock
Intake:	Jackson Racing
Throttle body:	Stock vs. 65mm
Air intake:	Stock vs. JR Air Intake
Filter:	Stock vs. Cone
Maf:	Stock vs. JR Custom
Header:	Stock Exhaust Manifold
Exhaust:	Stock
Injectors:	Stock 19 lbs./hr. vs. 30 lbs./hr.
Turbo:	NA
Blower:	Jackson Racing M45
Boost level:	5-6 psi vs 7-8 psi
Management:	Stock ECU
Fuel pump:	Stock
Intercooler:	NA
Nitrous:	No

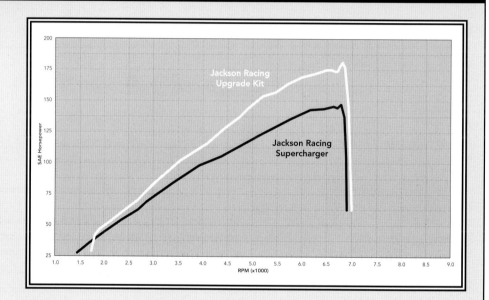

If you want to increase the power output of your supercharged Zetec motor, look no further than the inlet system. Of course a little extra boost pressure always helps the situation.

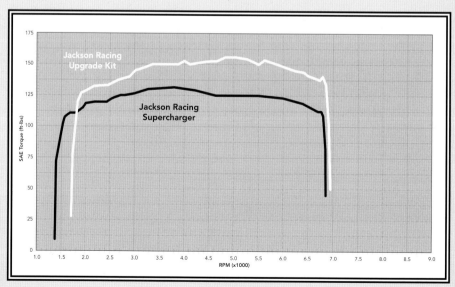

The gains offered by the upgrade kit from Jackson Racing were substantial. The peak-to-peak torque difference was 25 ft-lbs, but the largest difference was as high as 30 ft-lbs.

This Jackson Racing Focus was subjected to the upgrade package.

Test 3: Modified Zetec vs. Jackson Racing M62 Supercharger

Engine Specifications

Block:	Stock
Crank:	Stock
Rods:	Stock
Pistons:	Stock
Head:	Stock
Valves:	Stock
Cams:	Stock
Sprockets:	Stock
Intake:	Jackson Racing
Throttle body:	65mm
Air intake:	Custom 3-inch
Filter:	Cone
Maf:	ProM
Header:	Focus Sport Long Tube
Exhaust:	Borla
Injectors:	30 lbs./hr.
Turbo:	NA
Blower:	Jackson Racing M62
Boost level:	8-9 psi
Management:	Stock ECU
Fuel pump:	Stock
Intercooler:	NA
Nitrous:	No

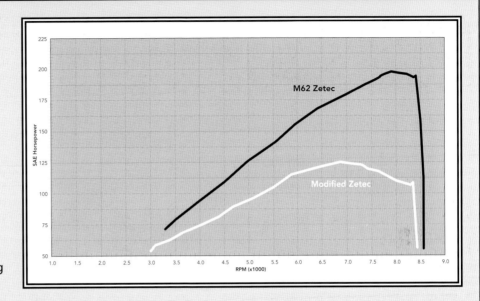

The Jackson Racing supercharger kit for the 2.0L Zetec Focus is impressive, but this prototype kit included the larger M62 supercharger in place of the smaller M45. Bolting on the bigger blower upped our power from 123 wheel horsepower to 196 hp.

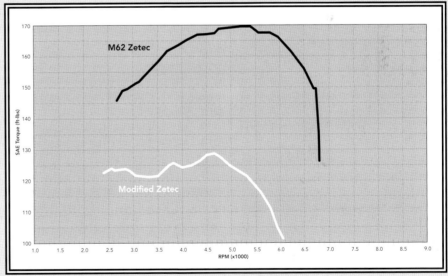

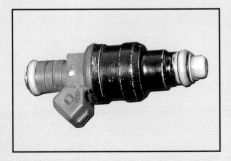

The installation included 30 pound injectors and a recalibrated ProM mass air meter.

Do you think you might feel an extra 60 ft-lbs of torque? The big blower excelled in producing power on this modified Zetec motor.

Test 3
Modified Zetec versus Jackson Racing M62 Supercharger

This next test involved installing a Jackson Racing supercharger on the author's own modified 2.0L Zetec motor. The supercharger was the start of a project vehicle (ZX3-GT) for *Muscle Mustangs & Fast Fords* magazine. The idea was to build a Focus capable of running head to head with a stock 4.6L Mustang GT; that meant coaxing 13-second time slips from the 2.0L Focus.

Knowing we were going to need some serious horsepower, we elected to install the larger M62 supercharger in place of the smaller M45 unit used in the standard Jackson Racing Focus kit. Rather than spin the smaller blower to the point where it became terribly inefficient, we chose to install the larger blower in the hopes that we could get the power without resorting to excessive boost and/or blower speed. The bigger blower required a dedicated intake manifold, something Jackson Racing machined up to accept the revised bolt pattern and larger blower discharge. Though it took more than just the supercharger, in the end, we were successful with the project, as the daily-driven Focus was able to run high 13s once we got the clutch to handle the added power.

Before installing the M62 supercharger, the Zetec motor featured an underdrive crank pulley (removed when we installed the supercharger), Focus Sport long-tube headers and a Borla exhaust. Additional mods included a Focus Sport flex pipe, Focus central

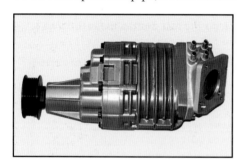

Test 2: The Jackson Racing supercharger kit utilized the M45 Eaton Roots (positive displacement) supercharger to provide immediate boost response.

Test 2: Adding the air intake improvements and increasing the boost pressure slightly resulted in a serious gain in power.

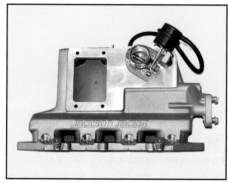

Test 3: The prototype kit installed on the author's 2001 Focus included this larger M62 supercharger. The bigger blower provided more power potential than the standard M45.

Test 3: The M62 bolted onto a revised intake that featured the necessary (larger) opening.

65mm throttle body, and custom air intake featuring the stock mass air meter. In this configuration, the Zetec motor produced 124 wheel horsepower. Adding the M62 supercharger, 30 lbs./hr. injectors, and ProM mass air meter increased the power peak to 197 wheel horsepower. At this power level the boost gauge was showing 8-9 psi at 6750 rpm. The torque peak jumped from 129 ft-lbs to 170 ft-lbs. More importantly than the gain in peak torque was the consistent increase in torque production across the rev range. To say that the difference between the mildly modified normally aspirated motor and the supercharged version was night and day is somewhat of an understatement. No longer was the Focus fair game for any VTEC-motored Honda willing to pick a fight. With some boost, the Focus easily dispatched all but the mightiest of normally aspirated VTEC-motored Hondas.

Test 4
Stock SVT versus
Jackson Racing Supercharger

When the Special Vehicle Team (SVT) introduced the SVT version of the Focus, enthusiasts really took notice. If there was one thing the stock ZX3 Zetec Focus was missing, it was power. Usually given high marks for its handling, creature comforts and economy, the stock Zetec Focus was never given praise for its wicked acceleration. With only 130 horsepower to motivate 2500 pounds (or more), the standard Focus was hopelessly outgunned against the current crop of imports. All that changed when the gang at SVT decided to try their hand at import fighting. Not only did they address the power issue by installing a sweetheart of a 2.0L motor, replete with higher compression, wilder cam timing, and even a dual-stage intake manifold (a la Acura Integra GSR), they

Test 4: The supercharged SVT motor produced 204 horsepower at the wheels, up from just 147 horsepower in stock trim.

Test 4: One nice thing about the SVT motor was that it came equipped with a larger throttle body.

Test 4: Stock SVT vs. Jackson Racing Supercharger

Engine Specifications

Block:	Stock SVT
Crank:	Stock SVT
Rods:	Stock SVT
Pistons:	Stock SVT
Head:	Stock SVT
Valves:	Stock SVT
Cams:	Stock SVT
Sprockets:	Stock SVT
Intake:	Jackson Racing
Throttle body:	Stock SVT
Air intake:	Stock SVT
Filter:	Stock SVT
Maf:	Stock SVT
Header:	Stock SVT vs. Focus Central Long Tube
Exhaust:	SVT
Injectors:	Stock SVT
Turbo:	NA
Blower:	Jackson Racing
Boost level:	5 psi
Management:	Stock ECU + JR Fuel Controller
Fuel pump:	Stock
Intercooler:	NA
Nitrous:	No

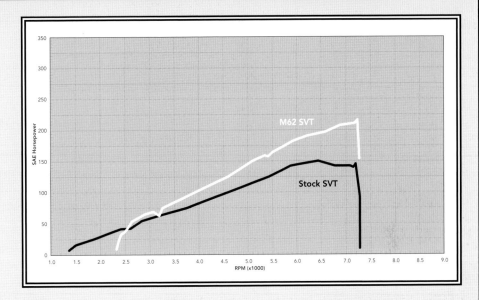

After installing the larger M62 supercharger kit on the 2.0L Zetec, Jackson Racing applied the same blower (with a revised intake) to the SVT motor. The result was a jump in peak power from 145 wheel horsepower to over 200 hp.

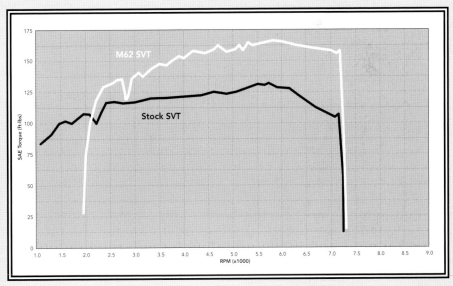

The supercharged SVT motor was equipped with the stock air box.

As with the Zetec motor, the torque curve produced by the Jackson Racing supercharger kit was plenty broad.

improved the braking and already impressive handling of the little Focus. The motor improvements upped the power ante from a lackluster 130 (flywheel) horsepower to an even 170 hp. More than most hot hatches currently on the road, the SVT represents a balanced attack of power, handling, and braking. Unfortunately, the competition does not stand still and soon 170 hp just wasn't going to cut it out on the mean streets. Enter Jackson Racing.

Since they had already produced an impressive kit for the standard Zetec Focus, it was only a matter of time before Jackson Racing got their hands on an SVT version to work their magic. Having supercharged a number of dif-

Test 5: Remove Boost Reference Line
Jackson Racing Supercharged Zetec

Engine Specifications

Block:	Stock
Crank:	Stock
Rods:	Stock
Pistons:	Stock
Head:	Stock
Valves:	Stock
Cams:	Stock
Sprockets:	Stock
Intake:	Jackson Racing
Throttle body:	65mm
Air intake:	Custom 3-inch
Filter:	Cone
Maf:	ProM
Header:	Focus Sport Long Tube
Exhaust:	Borla
Injectors:	0 lbs./hr.
Turbo:	NA
Blower:	Jackson Racing M62
Boost level:	8-9 psi
Management:	Stock ECU
Fuel pump:	Stock
Intercooler:	NA
Nitrous:	No

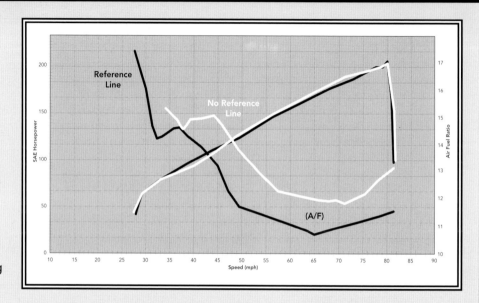

Removing the boost reference line to the pressure transducer on the fuel rail resulted in a shift in the air/fuel curve. The motor (as expected) leaned out and produced more power. Note that the lean condition became severe near 6,000 rpm (75 mph).

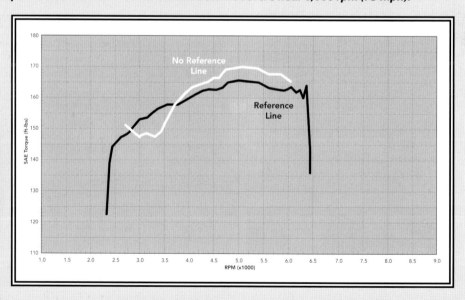

The motor was run with the boost reference attached to the pressure transducer.

Changing the air/fuel mixture by a full air/fuel point had a positive effect on the torque curve, but the lean condition near 6,000 rpm would have to be cured for daily driving. These air/fuel irregularities are why a stand-alone management system can be so useful to produce the optimum power (and air/fuel) curve.

ferent Honda/Acura motors of similar displacement and power output, not to mention their own research and development with the big blower on the stan-dard Zetec motor, Jackson Racing knew the M45 supercharger just wasn't going to get the job done on the high-horse-power SVT version. To that end, they configured a kit using the larger M62 Eaton supercharger. The benefit of using the larger M62 supercharger was the ability to slow the blower speed down (relative to the smaller M45) to produce a desired boost (and power) level.

Running the SVT Focus on the DynoJet resulted in 145 wheel horsepower. Adding the Jackson Racing supercharger kit (at just 5 psi) increased the power output to over 200 wheel horsepower. While 145 wheel horsepower is pretty respectable, you'll feel a lot safer pulling up to a stoplight against a VTEC motor if you're packing another 55-60 horsepower. As always, the 200+ wheel horsepower comes with full emissions certification.

Test 5
Remove Boost Reference Line-Jackson Racing Supercharged Zetec

This test was run to demonstrate the effect of boost referencing the pressure transducer. The vast majority of early (pre OBD-II) fuel-injected motors utilized a return-style fuel system. These fuel systems incorporated a fuel pump (usually in the fuel tank), fuel filter, fuel rail, and external fuel pressure regulator. The excess fuel from the fuel pressure regulator was returned to the fuel tank via a return line. Modern fuel systems, such as the one employed by Ford on the Focus (both Zetec and SVT) are quite different. These non-return fuel systems do not incorporate an external fuel pressure regulator, but instead rely on a pressure transducer located on the fuel rail to let the computer know what pressure is currently employed in the system. The pressure is controlled by the computer by modulating the pulse width of the fuel pump (not unlike pulsing a fuel injector to supply fuel). The pressure transducer on the fuel rail recognizes both vacuum and boost pressure, and the computer adjusts the fuel pressure in accordance with the changes seen by the transducer.

In the early (return-style) fuel systems, boost referencing the external regulator brought an increase in fuel pressure to offset the boost pressure. Fuel pressure must increase with boost pressure or the relative fuel flow will drop off. Imagine a situation when you try to run 40 psi of fuel pressure and 40

Test 5: The motor was run again without the boost reference, resulting in a dramatic change in the air/fuel mixture.

psi of boost pressure. The result would be no fuel flow. Lucky for us, the pressure transducer works in much the same way as the older fuel pressure regulators, in that the fuel pressure is increased (by the computer) when the transducer indicates the presence of boost pressure. To put this theory to the test, we ran our Zetec test motor equipped with a Jackson Racing supercharger (at 9 psi) with and without a boost reference line to the pressure transducer. As we see by the accompanying graph, removing the reference line actually increased the power output somewhat, but the air/fuel curve really tells the story. Equipped with 30-pound injectors (and meter), removing the boost reference line resulted in a dangerous lean condition, especially near the end of the rev range. Adding the boost pressure to the reference line resulted in an increase in fuel pressure and a much safer mixture. Of course all of this is predicated on the fact that the fuel pump is able to supply the necessary fuel flow at the elevated pressure.

Test 6
Effect of Blower Pulley/Boost PressureJackson Racing Supercharged Zetec

As has been mentioned time and time again, the great thing about forced induction, whether it be a turbo or a blower, is the ease of increasing the power output. In either case, simply increasing the boost pressure will likely result in additional power. The caveat is that increasing boost pressure will only work if sufficient airflow potential exists from

either the turbo or (in this case) the supercharger. If the turbo and/or supercharger are tapped out in terms of flow potential, then attempts at increasing the boost pressure will result in little or no power gain and can even result in a power loss. It is also important to note that more boost is not always the answer when it comes time to improve power. The most desirable approach is to improve power while reducing the boost pressure. This can be accomplished by improving the power output of the motor irrespective of the supercharger. Performance components such as aftermarket cam profiles (like the stage 1 Crane units employed on the test motor), ported cylinder heads, and free-flowing exhaust all help improve the power output without resorting to additional boost pressure. In fact, adding any one of these components will likely reduce the boost (more pronounced on a supercharged motor) while improving the power.

While improving the normally aspirated power is most desirable, most Focus owners will take the easy way out and simply go for more boost. To demonstrate what is possible with a Jackson Racing supercharger on a mildly modified motor, we selected three different supercharger pulleys and subjected the blown Zetec to different boost levels. The first supercharger pulley measured 3.4-inches in diameter and produced 8-8.5 psi. The motor produced 209 horsepower at the wheels. The next blower pulley measured 3.2 inches. The increase in blower speed increased the boost pressure to just over 10 psi, and the peak power rose to 220. The final 3.0-inch blower pulley increased the

Test 6: Changing the boost supplied by the blower was a simple matter of changing the size of the blower pulley.

Test 6: Effect of Blower Pulley/Boost Pressure
Jackson Racing Supercharged

Engine Specifications

Block:	Stock
Crank:	Stock
Rods:	Stock
Pistons:	Stock
Head:	Focus Central Ported
Valves:	Stock
Cams:	Crane Stage 1 206/210
Sprockets:	AEM
Intake:	Jackson Racing
Throttle body:	65mm
Air intake:	Custom 3-inch
Filter:	Cone
Maf:	ProM
Header:	Focus Sport Long Tube
Exhaust:	Borla
Injectors:	36 lbs./hr.
Turbo:	NA
Blower:	ackson Racing M62
Boost level:	8-12 psi
Management:	Stock ECU
Fuel pump:	Stock
Intercooler:	NA
Nitrous:	No

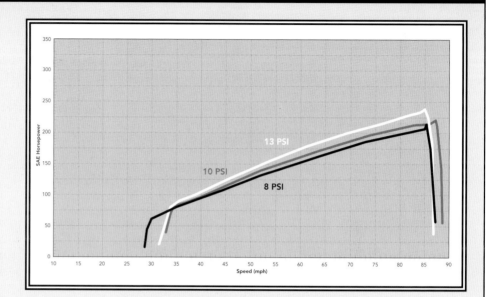

Installing any type of forced induction on your Focus allows you to dial in the horsepower by adjusting the boost pressure. Stepping down in blower pulley size result in boost pressures reaching 8, 10, and 13 psi. The difference between 8psi and 13 psi resulted in a peak power increase of a solid 30 hp.

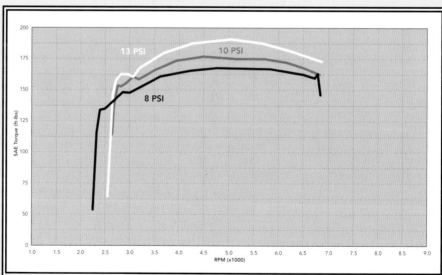

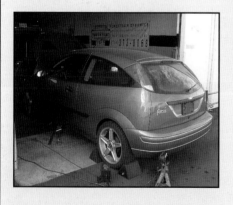

On the dyno, the boost improved the power output across the board.

One great thing about adding boost is that the power gains are present across the board. Adding boost increased the average torque production, something that would greatly improve acceleration.

boost pressure to 12.5-13.0 psi and the peak power to 237 hp. Note not only the gain in peak power but also the consistent gain throughout he rev range. As expected of an increase in boost pressure, the extra power was available from the moment you open the throttle. Remember though, there is a limit to how far you can take additional boost pressure. Running 12-13 psi without an intercooler required race fuel, something not ideal for daily street use.

UNDER PRESSURE

THE TECHNOLOGY OF TURBOCHARGING

Nothing transforms a motor quite like the addition of forced induction. Take even the mildest motor and add 6-7 psi of boost and suddenly the motor feels like it is ready to go out and kick some ass. In the case of the 2.0L Zetec motor, the transformation is quite remarkable. Though the Zetec will never be confused with a VTEC, adding a turbo kit (like the F-Max system) to a stock or mild combination will result in not only some serious horsepower, but (more importantly) some serious torque production. The emphasis Ford put on low-speed power production actually does wonders for a turbocharger. The low-speed power production provides plenty of exhaust energy to spin the turbo, thus boost is present at a very low engine speed. Where many motors (VTEC included) have to wait for the turbo to come on, the boosted Zetec owner can enjoy boost as low as 2,300 rpm if the turbo is sized properly. The benefit of having boost build quickly is something called torque. In addition to producing 188-192 wheel horsepower, a turbo Zetec will also produce over 200 ft-lbs of torque. It is this torque that allows part-throttle motoring around slower traffic and effortless merging up to freeway speeds.

Though both provide the airflow to dramatically increase the power output of a motor (we see this additional air-flow as boost pressure), superchargers and turbochargers differ in their approach. Each type has strengths and weaknesses, but the main difference is in their drive mechanisms. Superchargers (either positive displacement or centrifugal) are driven off the crank. Being mechanically coupled to the engine, the response rate of the supercharger, if not the boost pressure, is directly coupled to

the engine. Turbos, on the other hand, rely on exhaust flow to spin a turbine wheel. This turbine wheel is connected to a compressor wheel. The exhaust energy fed to the turbine spins the compressor which in turn provides airflow (boost) to the motor. The potential problem with the turbo is that a sufficient amount of exhaust energy must be present to spin the compressor. The time

If you are looking for ultimate horsepower, look no further than a turbocharged Zetec motor. This modified Focus Central Zetec motor featured an Innovative Turbo system designed by Kenny Duttweiler.

Test 1: The heavy Escape is certainly a candidate for the additional torque produced by a turbo motor.

Test 1: For our testing, the Gude turbo kit produced just 5 psi and ran without an intercooler.

between when the throttle is mashed and boost becomes present on the boost gauge is referred to as turbo lag. This lag can be adjusted by sizing the turbo properly, although most applications will never match the boost response of a positive displacement supercharger.

While the response rate can be debated, the efficiency is where the turbo is head and shoulders above the Roots supercharger. Centrifugal superchargers offer similar efficiency to the turbo, but still require more power to drive. What this means is that at a given boost level, a turbo will provide a lower charge temperature and more mass (air) flow to produce more power. The turbo also offers the potential for greater boost pressure levels compared to the Roots blower. Roots blowers tend to become

very inefficient above 10 psi, but not so with a properly sized turbo. It is not uncommon to see 15 psi, 20 psi, and even 25 psi of boost (or more) from a dedicated turbo motor. This is especially true when attempting to produce big power with minimal displacement.

The power potential of a turbo is a function of the normally aspirated power and the boost pressure. If you have a 100-hp motor and want to make 200 horsepower, all you need to do is add 1 bar, or 14.7 psi of boost. Naturally, this is an approximation, but since the normally aspirated motor relies on 1 atmosphere of pressure to produce 100 horsepower, doubling the pressure to 2 atmospheres (14.7 psi of boost) will usually double the power output. Tripling the power would require 29.4 psi or two additional atmospheres (14.7 x 2). Things really get interesting when you increase the power output of the normally aspirated motor. By increasing the power output of the 100 hp motor to 150 horsepower (with cams, head, and intake), the same 14.7 psi used to up the power of the 100 hp motor to 200 hp will increase the 150 hp motor to 300 hp. The better the starting point (of the NA motor), the better the eventual power output of the turbo motor at any given boost level.

Test 1
Gude Performance Escape

You might be wondering what a 2001 Ford Escape is doing in a performance Focus book, but rest assured the Escape and Focus share one major component in common—: the 2.0L Zetec power plant. The Escape belonged to Gude Performance and was used as a test mule to prototype performance components, including a turbo kit. Naturally the turbo kit was also designed to fit the Zetec-powered Focus. The Gude turbo kit was unique in that unlike the F-Max and Innovative turbo kits, the Gude system retained the stock exhaust manifold. Rather than build a custom log-style manifold (like F-Max) or a dedicated tubular header (like Innovative), Gude simply fabricated a collector adapter to mount the turbo on the facto-

ry exhaust manifold. Given the fact that the factory exhaust manifold was constructed of stainless steel, it should hold up to the added heat cycling, though bracing might be employed to help support the additional weight of the turbo. The extra heat generated by restricting the exhaust flow with the turbo softens the tubular manifold; when you combine the leverage applied by the additional weight of the turbo, it can taxing the material and the welds.

Speaking of turbos, the Gude kit came with a Mitsubishi TD04. Unlike the F-Max and Innovative kits, the TD04 employed an internal waste gate. On our system, the waste gate was set to open at 5-6 psi. The management system consisted of the author's own 36-pound injectors and recalibrated ProM mass air meter. The combination worked so well that Gude adopted the system for all of its kits. The meter/injector combination provided a tapering air/fuel curve that ended near 11.0:1 at 6,500 rpm. This type of tapering air/fuel curve is desirable for most street applications, as it ensures safety and minimizes the chance of detonation. It is possible to improve the power with a slightly leaner mixture, but care must be taken to avoid detonation. The ideal combination of total ignition advance, octane rating and air/fuel ratio is a delicate balance. Get even one of the variables wrong and your motor will let you know in a big way. It is best to be conservative on the tune, as the loss in power is very minimal compared to the potential destruction.

The Gude Escape produced 156 hp and 162 ft-lbs of torque at the wheels at 5-6 psi. Even more than the Focus, the heavy Escape was literally begging for additional torque. The Gude turbo kit provided just that.

Test 2
F-Max Turbo Zetec

The F-Max turbo kit supplied the power curve that Ford should have (and may in the very near future) put in the Zetec motor to begin with. Adding the F-Max turbo kit increased the power output of the Zetec motor from 112-hp to 188 hp at the wheels. The waste gate

Test 1: Gude Performance Escape

Engine Specifications

Block:	Stock
Crank:	Stock
Rods:	Stock
Pistons:	Stock
Head:	Stock 2.0L Zetec
Valves:	Stock
Cams:	Stock
Sprockets:	Stock
Intake:	Stock
Throttle body:	Stock
Air intake:	Custom Gude
Filter:	Cone
Maf:	Recalibrated ProM
Header:	Stock/Gude Collector Adapter
Exhaust:	Borla 1 7/8
Injectors:	36 lbs./h.r
Turbo:	Mitsubishi TD04H
Blower:	NA
Boost level:	5-6 psi
Management:	Stock ECU
Fuel pump:	Stock
Intercooler:	No, but available as option
Nitrous:	No

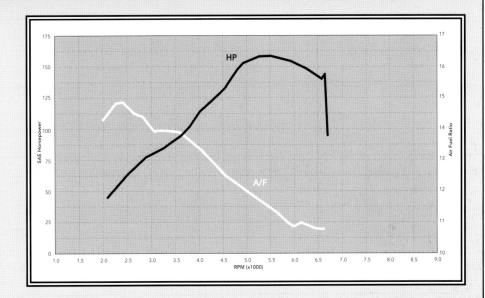

Running 5 psi of boost, the 2.0L Zetec produced 156 horsepower. Note the safe air/fuel curve produced by the 36-pound injectors and calibrated ProM meter.

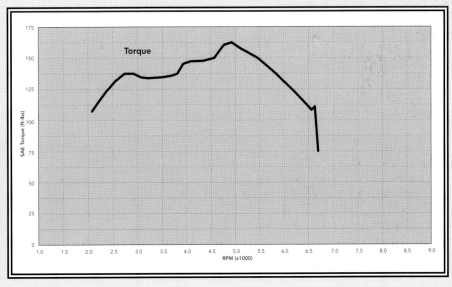

Running 5 psi of boost, the 2.0L Zetec produced 162 ft-lbs of torque.

The Escape shared the same Zetec motor as the Focus.

supplied with the kit was set to provide 6-7 psi of boost. Even more important than the peak power output of 188 hp was the torque production of 195 ft-lbs It is this impressive torque that literally throws you back in your seat when you mash on the gas, assuming your tires can find sufficient traction. The F-Max kit literally transformed the Zetec motor into something fun to drive. Full throttle was no longer required when making a passing maneuver, ditto for merging onto the freeway from the stoplights adjacent to California freeways. The F-Max kit included a Turbonetics T3/T4 hybrid turbo, an air-to-air intercooler, and Turbonetcis waste gate. F-Max also supplied all the necessary plumbing to connect the system, including an inlet tube to reposition the mass air meter.

Speaking of mass air meter, the F-Max turbo kit was run with a recalibrated mass air meter from ProM along with a set of 36-pound injectors from

Test 2: F-Max Turbo Zetec

Engine Specifications

Block:	Stock
Crank:	Stock
Rods:	Stock
Pistons:	Stock
Head:	Focus Central ported
Valves:	Stock
Cams:	Crane 210/206
Sprockets:	Focus Central
Intake:	Stock
Throttle body:	Stock
Air intake:	F-Max 2.5-inch
Filter:	Cone
Maf:	ProM
Header:	F-Max Turbo manifold
Exhaust:	Borla
Injectors:	36 lbs./hr.
Turbo:	Turbonetics/F-Max T3/T4 Hybrid
Blower:	NA
Boost level:	7 psi
Management:	Stock ECU
Fuel pump:	Stock
Intercooler:	F-Max
Nitrous:	No

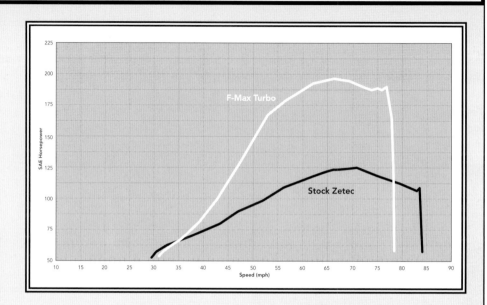

The F-Max turbo kit improved the power output of the Zetec motor by a whopping 70 horsepower.

The F-Max turbo kit proved both powerful and reliable over nearly 10,000 miles of driving.

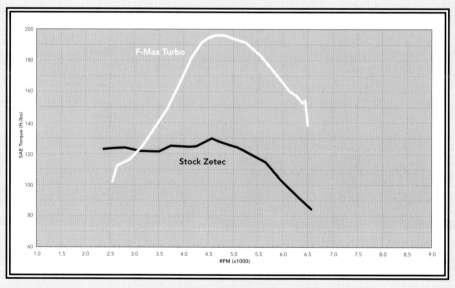

More importantly than the peak power output was the shape of the torque curve. This much torque made the Zetec motor a blast to drive.

RC Engineering. The combination was previously run with the Jackson Racing supercharger and Gude turbo motor with excellent results. With the ability of the turbo to supply additional air, some effort was necessary to supply the necessary fuel. The stock injectors were not going to get the job done. Neither was the stock mass air meter. Given the fact that Ford saw fit to equip the Zetec motor with a return-less fuel system, any manner of rising rate fuel regulator was out as a fuel-enrichment device. The cure was to install the ProM meter in place of the stock mass air and then run the larger 36-pound injectors. The injector/meter combo allowed the turbo to produce 14-15 psi before requiring more fuel. Check out the test on boost pressure to see how well the F-max kit performed at higher power levels.

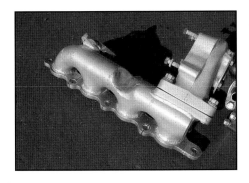

Test 2: The F-Max kit included a sturdy log-style manifold. The design helped improve response to the turbo.

Test 2: Though probably overkill at just 7 psi, the air-to-air intercooler was a welcome component once we cranked up the boost.

Test 3
F-Max Turbo Zetec
Effect Of Boost

One of the best things about forced induction is the ability to literally "dial up" additional horsepower at will. Obviously there is a limit to how much extra power is available, but as we were to find out, the F-Max turbo kit had plenty more power to offer. After running the F-Max kit at 7 psi, naturally we wanted more. The 36-pound injectors and meter were sufficient to supply the fuel needs, so we increased the boost pressure with a Turbo XS manual boost controller. At each level, we kept an eye on the air/fuel curve via the DynoJet. It should also be noted that the stock clutch and pressure plate assembly were no match for the extra power offered by the turbo system, so plan on installing a good clutch to harness all the turbo power. Before running the motor beyond 7 psi, we actually turned down the boost to just 5 psi by

Test 3: The Turbo XS manual boost controller was used to alter the signal to the waste gate to increase the boost pressure.

switching the boost reference line from the intake manifold to a fitting on the turbo. By swapping the position of the waste gate reference line, the waste gate saw a slightly higher boost reading at the turbo than in the manifold. The result was a drop in boost from 7 psi to 5 psi. Running just 5 psi, the motor produce 179 horsepower.

After upping the boost pressure back to 7 psi, the power climbed to 192 wheel horsepower, a slight gain over our initial runs. Credit a cooler intercooler or engine temperature for the difference. Using the Turbo XS controller, the boost was upped to just under 9 psi, where the motor produced 217 horsepower. Upping the boost further to 11 psi brought 227 horsepower, while 12 psi resulted in 241 wheel horsepower. Running 14-15 psi resulted in 270 horsepower and it was at this point that the air/fuel curve began to get lean near the end of the run. The air/fuel mixture was

Test 3: On the dyno, the power improved dramatically as we increased the boost. Remember, that it is critical to have sufficient fuel and to avoid detonation when increasing boost pressure.

nearing 13.0:1, way too lean for a turbo motor. The cure was to install a set of 72-pound injectors and a Pectel engine management system before we could successfully crank the boost beyond 15 psi. Check out the chapter on engine buildups to see what happened when we cranked up the boost to 18-19 psi. Even at 15 psi and 270 wheel horsepower the Focus motor was plenty stout. If traction was available, figure on running easy 12s with this setup.

Test 4
Innovative Turbo Zetec .48 vs.
.63 A/R Ratio

One way to tune the power curve of a turbo motor is by altering the A/R ratio of the turbine housing. Technically speaking, the A/R ratio refers to the area of the internal passages in the turbine housing divided by the radius or dis-

Test 4: Changes in A/R ratio can improve the response rate of the turbo, but expect to trade response for maximum power potential.

Test 4: The Innovative turbo system was used in conjunction with the F-Max air-to-air intercooler for the A/R ratio test.

Test 3: F-Max Turbo Zetec
Effect Of Boost

Engine Specifications

Block:	Stock
Crank:	Stock
Rods:	Stock
Pistons:	Stock
Head:	Focus Central ported
Valves:	Stock
Cams:	Crane 210/206
Sprockets:	Focus Central
Intake:	Stock
Throttle body:	Stock
Air intake:	F-Max 2.5-inch
Filter:	Cone
Maf:	ProM
Header:	F-Max Turbo manifold
Exhaust:	Borla
Injectors:	36 lbs./hr.
Turbo:	Turbonetics F-Max T3/T4 Hybrid
Blower:	NA
Boost level:	5-14 psi
Management:	Stock ECU
Fuel pump:	Stock
Intercooler:	F-Max
Nitrous:	No

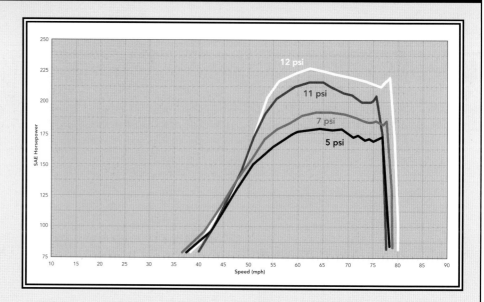

The great thing about a turbo motor is the ability to crank up the boost. Using a ProM meter and 36-pound injectors, we were able to dial up the power from 180 hp to 227 hp by increasing the boost from 5 psi to 11 psi.

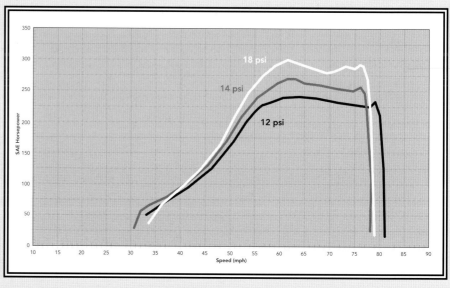

The boost pressure on the F-Max kit was controlled by this Tial waste gate.

Even more power was available from the F-max kit, though we had to replace the injectors and management system to reach 300 wheel horsepower.

tance between the center of the turbine wheel and the center of the internal passage. The turbine housing is really nothing more than a tapering (cone-shaped) tube wrapped around an impeller wheel. The exhaust gases flow through the cone, speeding up as the cone tapers. The speeding exhaust is directed to the tips of the turbine wheel, causing it to spin. Both the internal dimension (A) and the leverage applied by the distance from the center of the turbine wheel (R) change the response of the turbo. In some cases they can even change the potential power output, but changes in A/R that affect peak power output indicate that you are nearing the flow limit of the turbo. The A/R ratio is generally stamped or cast into the turbine housing. While the technical aspects are not as important, remember that smaller (numerical) A/R ratios improve turbo response but may limit top-end power production. Larger A/R ratios do just the opposite.

To illustrate the effect of changes in A/R ratio, I set up a test using the Innovative turbo system on a modified Zetec motor. The motor was run on the Dyno-Jet chassis dyno with the only change being the A/R ratio of the turbine housing. Though this particular test resulted in some definite differences in the power curve, many times a similar change in A/R ratio results in no change in power. This case was a textbook example of changes in A/R ratio. The modified turbo Zetec motor was run first with an Innovative T04E-46 turbo equipped

Test 4: Innovative Turbo Zetec .48 versus .63 A/R Ratio

Engine Specifications

Block:	Stock
Crank:	Stock
Rods:	Stock
Pistons:	Stock
Head:	Focus Central ported
Valves:	Stock
Cams:	Crane 210/206
Sprockets:	Focus Central
Intake:	Stock
Throttle body:	Focus Central 65mm
Air intake:	Custom 3-inch
Filter:	Cone
Maf:	ProM
Header:	Innovative Tubular Turbo Header
Exhaust:	Borla
Injectors:	72 lbs./hr.
Turbo:	Innovative T04E-46
Blower:	NA
Boost level:	20 psi
Management:	Pectel ECU
Fuel pump:	Stock with Kenne Bell Boost-a-Pump
Intercooler:	Vortech Aftercooler (air-to-water)
Nitrous:	No

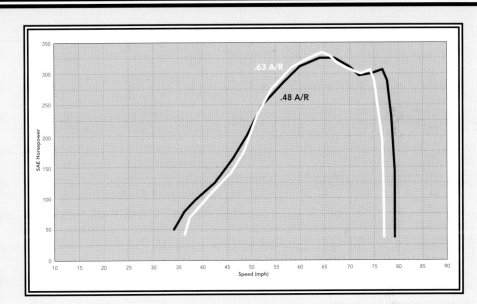

Changing the A/R ratio from .48 to .63 slowed the spool up but slightly increased the peak power offered by the Innovative T04E-46 turbo.

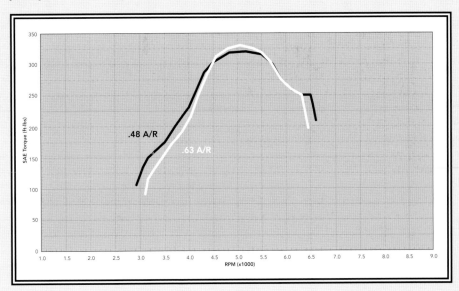

The torque curve tells a similar story, with the smaller A/R ratio offering improved torque thanks to a quicker spool-up.

Test 5: 365-hp Innovative Turbo Zetec

Engine Specifications

Block:	Stock
Crank:	Stock
Rods:	Stock
Pistons:	Stock
Head:	Focus Central ported
Valves:	Stock
Cams:	Crane 210/206
Sprockets:	Focus Central
Intake:	Stock
Throttle body:	Focus Central 65mm
Air intake:	Custom 3-inch
Filter:	Cone
Maf:	roM
Header:	Innovative Tubular Turbo Header
Exhaust:	Borla
Injectors:	72 lbs./hr.
Turbo:I	Innovative T04E-46
Blower:	NA
Boost level:	24psi
Management:	Pectel Stand Alone ECU
Fuel pump:	Stock with Kenne Bell Boost-a-Pump
Intercooler:	Vortech Aftercooler (air-to-water)
Nitrous:	No

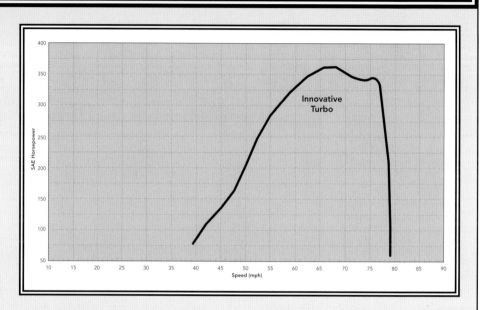

Adding the Innovative turbo system to a modified Zetec resulted in a peak reading of 364 horsepower.

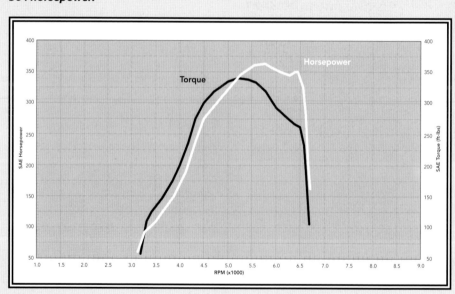

Check out the impressive torque curve offered by the turbocharged combination. The motor exceeded 300 ft-lbs from 4500 rpm to 6000 rpm.

with a .48 A/R ratio and then again with a .63 ratio housing. The .48 housing improved the low-speed response, but the .63 housing allowed the motor to produce more peak power. The differences were small (7 hp out of a total of 330 hp), but the two graphs showed a decided change in the way the turbo responded. The test shows that it is possible to tune your turbocharged combination by altering the A/R ratio, just don't expect miracles. The right A/R ratio will not make up for the wrong turbo selection.

Test 5
365-hp Innovative Turbo Zetec

This test was interesting in that it illustrated the strength of the stock Zetec short block. It has been mentioned elsewhere in the book that the Zetec

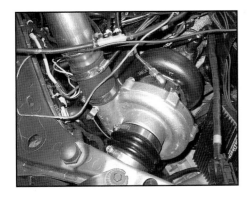

Test 4: The Innovative Turbo system was first run with a T04E-46 turbo.

motors earned a misguided reputation for having weak internals. The powdered metal rods were said to be a weak link, but both the 8,300-rpm stock-block race motor (see 12-second engine buildup) and this 365-hp turbo motor illustrate that the truth is otherwise. It is likely that the early failures (if they existed) were the cause of poor tuning.

Test 5: We eventually relied on a Vortech air-to-water After Cooler to reach 365 wheel horsepower with the stock short block and T04E-46 turbo.

Test 5: The T04E-46 turbo from Innovative offered plenty of power potential.

Running 10 psi of boost with a factory timing curve on low-octane fuel will likely bring detonation easily capable of holing a piston or snapping a rod. The same goes for attempting to run a turbo motor with stock injectors or without some form of fuel management. No motor ever built will withstand sustained detonation. The key to engine longevity is proper tuning, much more than spending big money on forged internals. Obviously at some point, it is necessary to pop for good components, just don't think that will overcome poor tuning. If the air/fuel and timing are spot on, forged internal components will allow you to make serious power.

For this test, the modified Zetec motor (mildly ported head, stage 1 Crane cams, and ported intake) was equipped with an Innovative Turbo kit that featured a custom tubular header. The stainless steel header worked in conjunction with an Innovative T04E-46 turbo and a Vortech air-to-water Aftercooler. The exhaust consisted of a custom down tube flowing into a Borla 2.5-inch cat-back exhaust. The boost pressure was increased using a Turbo XS manual boost controller and at the elevated boost levels, we fed the After Cooler with ice water. The management system consisted of a Pectel stand-alone computer and 72-pound per hour injectors working with a Kenne Bell Boost-a-Pump augmented fuel pump. The tank was filled with Union 76 118 Pro Stock race fuel in order to keep detonation at bay, as we knew there was no room for error with the factory pistons and rods. After cranking the boost to 24 psi, the

Test 5: The Innovative turbo featured a stainless steel header to feed the turbo.

Test 6: With the line off, the air/fuel leaned out dramatically, indicating that the fuel pressure is increased in relation to boost pressure (just like the older regulators used on return fuel systems).

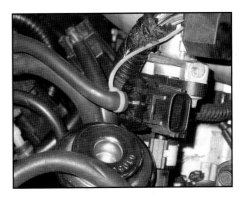

Test 6: This test involved testing the effect (on the air/fuel curve) of removing the boost reference line to the pressure transducer.

Innovative Turbo Zetec (stock short block) pumped out 365 wheel horsepower and 347 ft-lbs of torque. We knew the Innovative turbo had more to offer and additional power was likely available with a revised intake manifold (see intake comparison), but we were happy that the stock short block survived all the abuse (30-40 runs over 300 hp) and called it a day.

Test 6
Boost Referenced Pressure Transducer – F-Max Turbo Zetec

Ford saw fit to equip the Zetec and SVT motors with a return-less fuel system. In the old days (just a couple of years ago), fuel systems were equipped with a fuel pump, rail, regulator, and return line. The fuel was fed to the rails,

Test 6: Boost Referenced Pressure Transducer F-Max Turbo Zetec

Engine Specifications

Block:	Stock
Crank:	Stock
Rods:	Stock
Pistons:	Stock
Head:	Focus Central ported
Valves:	Stock
Cams:	Crane 210/206
Sprockets:	Focus Central
Intake:	Stock
Throttle body:	Stock
Air intake:	F-Max 2.5-inch
Filter:	Cone
Maf:	ProM
Header:	F-Max Turbo manifold
Exhaust:	Borla
Injectors:	36 lbs./hr.
Turbo:	Turbonetics F-Max T3/T4 Hybrid
Blower:	NA

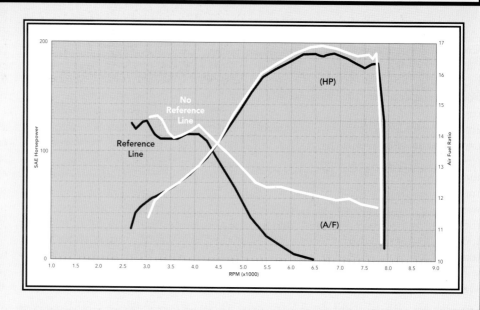

Removing the boost reference line to the pressure transducer dramatically leaned out the air/fuel mixture. In this case, leaning out the mixture resulted in a gain in power, but this should not be attempted at elevated boost levels.

Boost level:	5-14 psi		Intercooler:	F-Max
Management:	Stock ECU		Nitrous:	No
Fuel pump:	Stock			

the pressure set by the regulator and the excess returned to the tank. This setup allowed aftermarket turbo and supercharger manufacturers to install what is best described as a rising rate fuel regula-

Test 6: The F-Max turbo system was called upon to perform numerous tests for this book.

tor. This system included a vacuum-boost reference line to increase the fuel pressure under boost. Unfortunately, the new return-less system does not provide for such fuel enrichment. The new system actually monitors the boost pressure using a pressure transducer in the fuel rail. The fuel pressure is controlled by the computer via pulse-width modulation of the fuel pump. If the computer senses excessive fuel pressure, then the pump is instructed to reduce the fuel flow. This all but negates any type of rising rate fuel pressure regulator.

The pressure transducer does however have a vacuum/boost line, which affects the system fuel pressure. The good news (for turbo and blower manufacturers and kit buyers) is that feeding the pressure transducer boost pressure will result in an increase in fuel pressure at a 1:1 rate with the boost. While not nearly as effective as a rising rate regula-

tor, the boost-referenced pressure transducer does at least allow the fuel pressure to increase with boost. When combined with a recalibrated meter and larger injectors, the result is an acceptable air/fuel curve. To demonstrate the effectiveness of boost-referencing the pressure transducer, we made back-to-back runs on the dyno with and without a boost line to the transducer. Though the power differed by 5-6 hp, the effect on the air/fuel curve was dramatic. Running at 7 psi (F-Max kit), the air/fuel curve was safely rich, dropping down to 10:1 (actually a tad too rich) out near 5,500 rpm. Removing the reference line leaned out the mixture by two full air/fuel points, to 12.0:1. The curve from 4,000 rpm to 5,500 rpm was well to the lean side of being safe, so make sure to have boost pressure feeding the transducer when you install your turbo or blower kit.

Test 7
Ken Duttweiller/Innovative Turbo (Modified Zetec)

This was actually the turbo system that started me down the path of building the 500-hp monster detailed in Chapter 8. After seeing the Innovative tubular header and revised turbo mounting position on Ken Duttweiler's Focus, I decided that I had to have one. Interestingly enough, Ken's kit did not employ an intercooler, something that should be considered mandatory to control charge temperature, and therefore the propensity toward detonation. The Innovative Turbo system on Ken's car was also running a stand-alone management system, a Pectel, at the time of our testing. The motor was pretty mild in terms of performance modifications, no wild cam timing or extensive head porting. Most of the modifications were

Test 7: The Kenney Duttweiler Focus was tested on the Borla DynoJet with excellent results. Naturally, the Focus was equipped with a stainless steel Borla exhaust.

done to increase longevity, such as the forged pistons and rods. Anyone who knows anything about Ken Duttweiler knows that he can build serious turbo power. Need 1,000 horsepower, 1,500 horsepower, or even 2,000 horsepower,

Test 7: The turbo motor relied on an Innovative/Duttweiler tubular header to feed the small turbo. Note the lack of an external waste gate or intercooler on this application.

Ken is the man you need to see. In the case of this particular test run on the Focus, the limiting factor was the small turbo he had installed at the time. Apparently I missed the big turbo by a week or so, and scheduling never

Test 7: Ken Duttweiller/Innovative Turbo (Modified Zetec)

Engine Specifications

Block:	Stock
Crank:	Stock
Rods:	Eagle
Pistons:	Forged
Head:	Ported
Valves:	Stock
Cams:	Stock
Sprockets:	Stock
Intake:	Fabricated Sheet Metal
Throttle body:	65mm Mustang
Air intake:	Custom
Filter:	Cone
Maf:	None
Header:	Duttweiller/Innovative
Exhaust:	Borla
Injectors:	42 lbs./hr.
Turbo:	Innovative T28
Blower:	NA
Boost level:	14 psi
Management:	Pectel
Fuel pump:	Stock
Intercooler:	None
Nitrous:	No

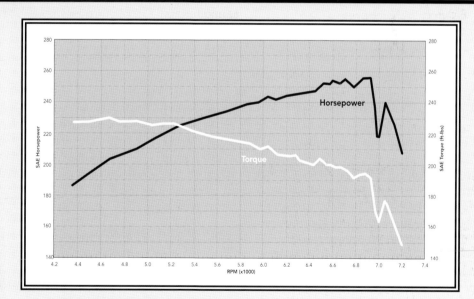

This is the power graph that got me started building the 500-hp turbo motor. Kenny Duttweiler built this turbo Focus motor using the same Innovative header system. Though impressive, the Focus motor was limited by a small turbo.

Test 7: The limiting factor in terms of horsepower was the small turbo run during testing.

allowed re-installation for testing. Even equipped with a tiny T28 turbo, the turbo Zetec produced 260 wheel horsepower at 13-14 psi. I can vouch for this, the car was a blast to drive in this configuration. (Thanks go out to Chris Kaufmann and the gang at Borla for helping us get the thing on the dyno!)

Test 8
Effect of Boost-Innovative Turbocharged Zetec

Boost pressure is a wonderful thing. The problem comes when you try to get too much of a good thing. Using our APEXi Super AVC Type R electronic waste gate controller, we increased the boost on our 500-hp turbo test motor. Not surprisingly, the motor responded with more power as we turned up the boost. With each pound of boost, the motor gained approximately 13-15 horsepower. Running 25 psi, the motor produced 463 horsepower. After upping the boost pressure in succession, the motor eventually produced 507 horsepower at 28 psi. The increase in power with boost is not surprising, but it does take several key components to allow it to function properly. Simply cranking up the boost can be a recipe for damage if you do not follow a few simple precautions.

The first precaution when cranking up the boost is to ensure that there is adequate fuel delivery to go along with the boost. The primary culprits here are injector sizing and fuel pump capacity, but things like fuel filters, fuel line and

even pump voltage can become important at these elevated power levels. The next thing to consider when running over 20 psi of boost is intercooling. It is not uncommon for the charge temperature to exceed 300, 350, or even 400 degrees at super-high boost levels. Naturally this super-heated inlet air can help spark detonation. We relied on an air-to-water intercooler and even ice water, once we reached 29 psi. Our fuel system included an Aeromotive fuel pump capable of supporting well over 700 horsepower at the high fuel pressure we were running, and our 72-pound injectors offered sufficient fuel to go to 550 horsepower when combined with the added fuel pressure. Adjusting the boost pressure via our APEXi controller was the easy part. Making sure all of the systems were ready for the additional boost was a bit tougher.

Test 9
Stock vs. Pectel Turbo System (Stock Zetec)

Obviously not every Focus owner is looking to build a 500-hp turbo motor. In truth, a 500-hp turbo motor really has no place on the street, but that doesn't mean you can't enjoy a turbo Zetec motor. Pectel, the company who designed the stand alone management systems for the Focus, decided to throw their hat into the turbo ring by building a dedicated, bolt-on turbo system for the 2.0L Zetec (and later SVT). The turbo system included a responsive T28 turbo equipped with an internal waste gate. Regulated to just 7 psi, the system still offered a front-mounted air-to-air

Test 8: This wild Innovative turbo motor was used to test the effectiveness of increasing boost pressure.

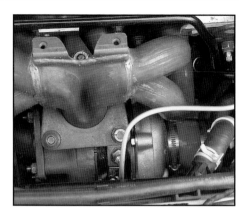

Test 9: Pectel designed a bolt-on turbo system for the 2.0L Zetec. In addition to the responsive T28 turbo, the turbo kit featured an air-to-air intercooler, 36-pound injectors and recalibrated mass air meter.

Test 9: One unique component of the Pectel system was that the turbo bolted directly to the stock exhaust manifold thanks to this trick turbine casting.

intercooler. Obviously Pectel knows that enthusiasts are inclined to crank up the boost beyond the preset level. The standard turbo system also comes with the necessary fueling system consisting of a set of 36-pound injectors and a recalibrated ProM mass air meter. The

Test 8: The APEXi Super AVC Type R electronic waste gate controller was used to keep accurate control over the boost.

Test 8: Effect of Boost
Innovative Turbocharged Zetec

Engine Specifications

Block:	Stock
Crank:	Stock
Rods:	Crower
Pistons:	Sean Hyland/JE
Head:	Focus Central (Extensively ported)
Valves:	1mm oversize
Cams:	Custom Crower
Sprockets:	Focus Central
Intake:	Ford Racing
Throttle body:	65mm
Air intake:	4-inch Custom
Filter:	4x12-inch K&N
Maf:	None
Header:	Innovative Tubular
Exhaust:	Borla
Injectors:	72 lbs./hr.
Turbo:	Innovative GT66
Blower:	NA
Boost level:	25-28 psi
Management:	Pectel
Fuel pump:	Aeromotive with custom return fuel system (Kenne Bell Boost-a-Pump)
Intercooler:	Vortech air-to-water Aftercooler
Nitrous:	No

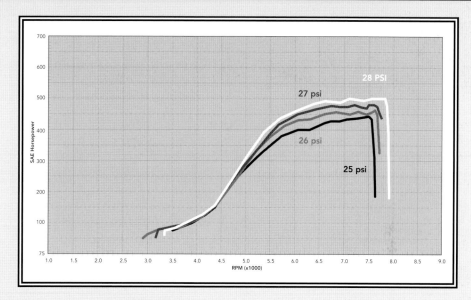

Using the APEXi Super AVC, we were able to increase the boost pressure to our fancy turbo Zetec. Upping the boost pressure increased the power peak from 463 hp (at 25 psi) to 507 hp (at 28 psi).

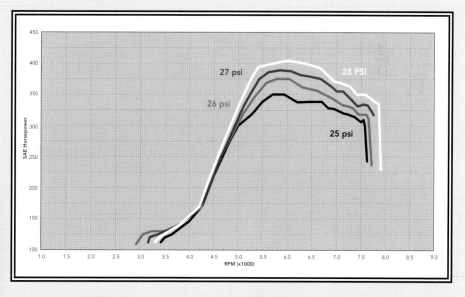

Imagine what a 2.0L Zetec that pumps out over 400 ft-lbs of torque feels like on the street. Upping the boost pressure increased the torque peak from 350 ft-lbs to over 400 ft-lbs.

combination provides a safe air/fuel mixture under boost, something critical to both performance and longevity.

As expected of the Pectel system at 7 psi, the turbo motor responded with plenty of horsepower and torque. The T28 turbo proved responsive, delivering boost as low as 2000 rpm. Regulated to just 7 psi, the Pectel turbo system managed to produced 191 horsepower and 204 ft-lbs of torque on the Zetec test motor. Running the motor on the dyno at 2,000 rpm resulted in an immediate gain in power over the stock motor. The power gains increased with boost pressure and rpm, until the turbo motor produced 191 horsepower at 5,400rpm. The torque curve was even more impressive, as the Pectel turbo motor exceeded 175 ft-lbs of torque from 3,200 rpm to 5,700 rpm. It is this lofty torque curve that made the turbo motor such a blast to drive. Adding 7 psi of boost from the Pectel turbo system felt like we just doubled the displacement. The motor could be driven like a big V6, such is the benefit of forced induction.

Test 9: Stock vs. Pectel Turbo System (Stock Zetec)

Engine Specifications

Block:	Stock
Crank:	Stock
Rods:	Stock
Pistons:	Stock
Head:	Stock
Valves:	Stock
Cams:	Stock
Sprockets:	Adj (max retard)
Intake:	Stock
Throttle body:	Focus Central 65mm
Air intake:	Pectel
Filter:	Cone
Maf:	ProM
Header:	Stock
Exhaust:	APEXi
Injectors:	310cc
Turbo:	T28
Blower:	NA
Boost level:	7 psi
Management:	Stock
Fuel pump:	Stock
Intercooler:	Pectel Air-to-air
Nitrous:	No

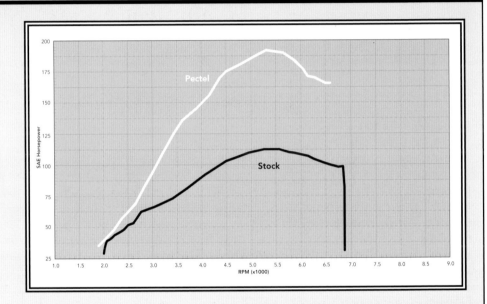

Compared to the stock Zetec motor, the Pectel turbo system offered a significant boost in power. Note that the power gains occurred as low as 2,000 rpm. The response offered by the Pectel turbo system was impressive.

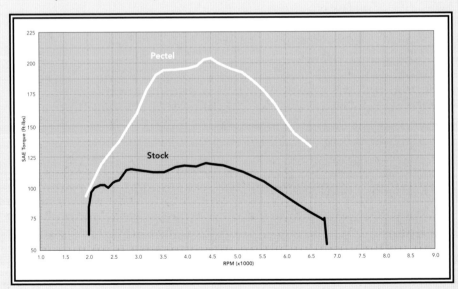

Pectel finished the prototype just before this book went to print. The production systems will feature powder-coated tubing and a ProM mass air meter.

Though we all talk about horsepower, the torque curve is what we actually enjoy on the street. From 2,000 rpm to redline, the Pectel turbo system offered significant torque gains. The small T28 turbo and use of the stock exhaust manifold and dedicated turbine casting resulted in impressive response and torque production.

MILD TO WILD

ZETEC ENGINE BUILDUPS

When it comes time to produce maximum power from a Zetec or SVT Focus, the best route is often a dedicated buildup. Sure, the normal bolt-ons will yield impressive results, but maximum power only comes from a dedicated combination of components working together as one cohesive unit. The intake runner length, head flow, and cam timing must be synchronized with the header primary length, and of course all this madness must be tuned properly to produce optimum results. Adding a turbo kit to an otherwise stock Zetec motor will result in an impressive gain in performance. Adding the same kit to a built motor featuring forged pistons, a ported head, and custom intake can double or triple the normally aspirated power output.

Such is the power potential of the proper combination of components.

It was obviously not possible to build every conceivable Zetec and SVT combination. In the end, I chose a number of buildups to represent what the average enthusiasts might attempt and combined this list with a few wilder efforts. Thus, the buildups range from a 192-hp street all-motor combo to a wild 500-hp turbo race motor. Sandwiched in between are a number of powerful performers, including a 13-second, 235-hp supercharged buildup, the Focus Central 12-second all-motor Zetec, and a 300-hp F-Max turbo motor. The buildups include power levels surpassing normal bolt ons. While a number could be considered dedicated race motors, a number can and were street driven on a daily

basis. In fact, both the 223-hp all-motor and 500-hp turbo buildups could probably be driven on a regular basis, but both required the use of the Pectel engine management system. I have driven street Foci equipped with the Pectel system with excellent results. I see no reason why the Focus Central all-motor combo or the 500-hp turbo motor could not be driven using the Pectel to tune the necessary street manners.

Test 1
190-hp Focus Central
Street Zetec

With the success of their stock-block race motor program, Focus Central decided to apply what they learned on the dyno to a street motor. Natural-

Maximum power sometimes requires building a dedicated motor. This chapter covers buildups ranging from 223-hp all-motor machines to a 514-hp monster turbo motor.

Test 1: 190-hp Focus Central Street Zetec

Engine Specifications

Block:	Stock Zetec
Crank:	Stock Zetec
Rods:	Stock Zetec
Pistons:	Stock Zetec
Head:	Focus Central ported & milled (.030)
Valves:	Stock
Cams:	Crower Stage 3
Sprockets:	Focus Central Adjustable
Intake:	Focus Central Composite
Throttle body:	Focus Central 65mm
Air intake:	Focus Central Cold Air
Filter:	Cone
Maf:	ProM w adjustable Optimizer
Header:	Focus Central 1.75-inch Race
Exhaust:	Focus Central 2.5-inch

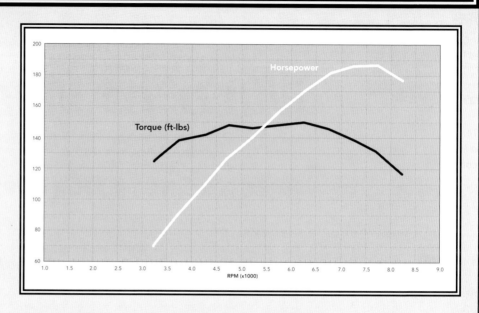

Though labeled a street motor, the 190-hp buildup from Focus Central offered impressive peak power and a broad torque curve. The 2.0L Zetec motor produced more than 140 ft-lbs of torque from 3800 rpm to 7000 rpm.

Injectors:	30 lbs./hr.			Chip
Turbo:	NA	Fuel pump:	Stock
Blower:	NA	Intercooler:	NA
Boost level:	NA	Nitrous:	No
Management:	Stock ECU with		

Test 1: This innocent looking Zetec motor pumped out nearly 190 wheel horsepower thanks to some massaging from Focus Central.

ly, a street motor and a race motor are two entirely different animals, despite (in this case) sharing a common stock Zetec short block. Street motors, by design, are full of compromises. The compromises are necessary in order to allow for everyday operation. Take reliability for instance. Daily drivers must be reliable, lest they leave you (or even worse a loved one) stranded on the side of the road (probably on your way to work). Race motors, on the other hand, need not start on the first crank of the key, as they are usually only operated within close proximity to the tools necessary to eventually bring them to life. While you might tolerate an erratic idle, poor fuel mileage, and excessive noise from your race motor, the same can't be said for your street car. It is these compromises that reduce the eventual power output of a street motor compared to a similar race motor.

Though compromised in terms of cam, compression, and head flow com-pared to their race motor, the 190-hp street motor represented a significant improvement in power compared to a stock Zetec. Not surprisingly, the

Test 1: This short-runner intake was used to shift the torque curve by more than 1000 rpm. The result was a dramatic increase in high-RPM power compared to the stock intake.

Test 1: The modified Zetec motor relied on a ProM mass air meter and Focus Central cold air intake system.

Test 1: On the chassis dyno, the Focus Central street motor produced 187 horsepower and 150 ft-lbs of torque.

Test 1: The air/fuel mixture was tuned using this Optimizer by ProM.

impressive power output required modifications to all of the major power components. Like most modern motors, there is not one single component restricting the power output. Ford, like most manufacturers, recognizes the importance of matching the components to produce an optimized package. All of the power components applied to the 2.0L Zetec motor were designed to produce a combination of driveability, emissions compliance, and a given power and torque curve. The end result was a motor that produced 130 flywheel horsepower or about 108 wheel horsepower. Bolt-on components can increase the power out-

put, but upping that power significantly requires major changes.

The changes to the 190-hp street motor included head porting, cam timing, and even a revised intake manifold, along with the usual array of bolt-ons. Working from the air-intake system back, the motor received a ram air intake system, complete with a fresh air source from the carbon fiber hood. The air intake fed a ProM mass air meter equipped with an adjustable optimizer to fine-tune the air/fuel mixture. Naturally, the motor received one of their own 65mm throttle bodies as well as a custom composite intake manifold. The manifold was designed to shift the torque curve in an effort to increase the usable rev range of the motor. The procedure is mentioned elsewhere in the book, but shifting the torque curve by 1000 rpm (without changing the peak torque number) can result in gains of 50-60 horsepower. Naturally the trade off inherent in producing more top-end power is a reduction in low-speed torque, but the trick is to optimize the power curve to produce a broad power band. The dual-runner intake used on the SVT version (and tested in chapter 2 on a Zetec motor) is a textbook example of attempting to produce a broad power band.

The short-runner intake fed a ported Zetec cylinder head. The reason for porting the cylinder head was to improve the airflow potential. The more air you can feed a motor, the more power it can produce. The stock Zetec head is somewhat restrictive, but the Focus Central porting improved the flow characteristics con-

siderably. Naturally this head did not receive the amount of attention applied to the race head, but the porting still improved the flow rate of both the intake and exhaust ports dramatically, while producing a very desirable intake-to-exhaust flow relationship. The head also received minor milling (.030) to slightly increase the static compression.

Since the head flowed so well, it was only natural to improve the cam lift by installing Crower Stage 3 cams. The Stage 3 cams offered 236 degrees of intake duration and .413 lift, 244 degrees of exhaust duration and .433 lift. As of this writing, Crower was in the process of revising their Zetec cam profiles. Typically a motor with the intake-to-exhaust flow relationship offered by the Zetec head (especially ported) will respond best to a dual-pattern profile favoring the intake. The Crower Stage 3s favored the exhaust, but according to information supplied to the author, that was in the process of changing.

In addition to the short-runner intake, ported cylinder head, and Crower Stage 3 cams, the 190-hp street motor also received a number of bolt-on performance mods allowing unrestricted breathing to the head/intake/cam combination. The bolt-ons included a 65mm throttle body, 1-3/4-inch (primary tube diameter) race header, off-road pipe, and 2.5-inch cat-back exhaust system. Naturally, the motor also received a set of adjustable cam sprockets to tune the Stage 3 cams. With the installation of the long-tube race header, it was necessary to ditch the catalytic converter. A ProM mass air meter was employed both to increase the airflow potential of the inlet system and to allow adjustability of the air/fuel mixture via a ProM Optimizer. The Optimizer allowed adjustment of the voltage curve supplied by the mass air meter (to the computer). Altering the mass air voltage signal to the computer resulted in changes in the air/fuel mixture. Once tuned properly, the combination pumped out 187 wheel horsepower at 7400 rpm and 150 ft-lbs of torque at 6000 rpm. In addition to nearly reaching 190 wheel horsepower, the combination offered a broad torque curve, besting 140 ft-lbs from 3800 rpm to 7000 rpm.

Test 2
13-Second Supercharged Zetec Buildup

We continue this chapter with a buildup originally performed for Muscle Mustangs & Fast Fords magazine entitled ZX3-GT. The idea was to build a Ford Focus capable of running head to head with a current 4.6L Mustang GT—thus the name ZX3-GT. In stock trim, a 2-valve 4.6L Mustang GT produced 260 horsepower, or roughly 235 wheel horsepower as measured on a DynoJet chassis dyno. In stock trim, a Mustang GT could be coaxed (if well driven) to run high 13s to low 14s in the 1/4-mile at somewhere near 99 miles per hour. Naturally the

Test 2: 13-Second Supercharged Zetec Buildup

Engine Specifications

Block:	Stock
Crank:	Stock
Rods:	Stock
Pistons:	Stock
Head:	Focus Central ported
Valves:	Stock
Cams:	Crane 210/206
Sprockets:	Focus Central
Intake:	Jackson Racing
Throttle body:	65mm
Air intake:	Custom 3-inch
Filter:	Cone
Maf:	ProM
Header:	Focus Sport Long Tube
Exhaust:	Borla
Injectors:	36 lbs./hr.
Turbo:	NA
Blower:	Jackson Racing M62
Boost level:	12-13 psi
Management:	Stock ECU
Fuel pump:	Stock
Intercooler:	NA
Nitrous:	No

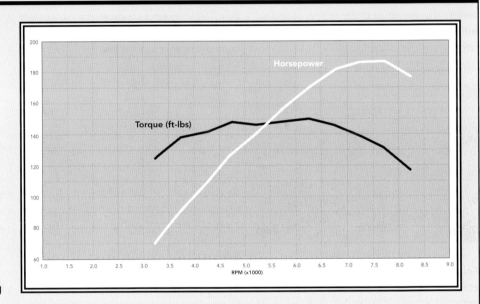

It took some doing, but I finally managed to coax 237 wheel horsepower out of my supercharged Zetec. The Jackson Racing kit featured an M62 supercharger running 12-13 psi of boost. The combination eventually pushed the Focus into the 13s.

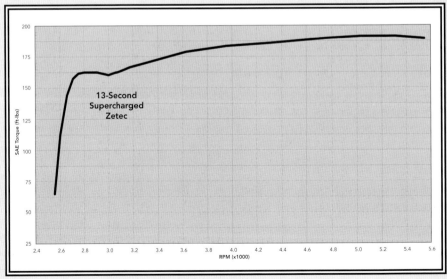

The supercharged combination produced a flat torque curve, bettering 175 ft-lbs from 3,500 rpm to 6,500 rpm.

The larger supercharger required an unrestricted inlet system consisting of a 65mm throttle body, 3-inch inlet tube and free-flowing cone filter.

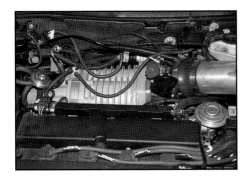

Test 2: The heart of the 13-second super-charged package was the Jackson Racing M62 supercharger. The larger super-charger allowed us to exceed 235 wheel horsepower on the modified Zetec.

Test 2: Focus Sport supplied a large-diam-eter tubular header for our supercharged motor. All the air forced into the motor must find a way out or power suffers.

Test 2: The torque produced by the super-charged motor easily exceeded the avail-able traction. Nursing the car off the line, we were eventually able to get the (full weight) street Focus well into the 13s at over 102 mph.

Mustang was significantly heavier than the Focus, so we figured that our goal should be to match the power output of the normally aspirated V8. Of course we recognized that there were other factors contributing to our acceleration rate,

Test 2: Naturally we tried a variety of dif-ferent pulley sizes to accomplish our power goal. Ultimately we employed a 3-inch blower pulley to produce 12-13 psi of boost.

namely gearing, traction (or lack there of), and even aerodynamics, though the effect would be most pronounced near the end of the run where the speed was greatest. Actually, our biggest hurdle would not be power but actually traction, as the front-wheel drive configuration of the Focus limited our 0-60-foot times, meaning we were giving the V8 Mustang a significant head start.

After running the gamut of minor bolt-ons, we finally decided it was going to take some serious forced induction to achieve our power goals. To that end, we decided to install a supercharger kit from Jackson Racing. Having seen the impressive results from our previous testing using the standard kit, we knew there was plenty of power waiting to be unleashed from a supercharged Zetec. We also recognized the limitations of the smaller M45 supercharger used in the standard Jackson Racing kit. Since we wanted to exceed 200 wheel horsepower by a significant margin, we decided to take Oscar Jackson up on his offer to run a (then new) prototype supercharg-er kit using the larger M62 supercharger. Having seen this larger M62 supercharg-er easily exceed 200 wheel horsepower on Honda/Acura VTEC applications, we knew that we were heading in the right direction. After installing the kit on the internally stock Zetec motor, the M62 supercharger increased the power output from 124 horsepower to 197 horsepower. Though a significant gain to be sure, we were still a long way from our goal of 235 wheel horsepower.

One of the great things about any form of forced induction (turbo or supercharging) is the ability to dial up the power output by increasing the boost pressure. In the case of the Jackson Racing supercharger, more boost (and power) was a simple matter of installing a smaller supercharger pulley. The instal-lation of a 3.0-inch blower pulley increased the boost pressure to 12-13 psi and increased the power output to 217 horsepower. While beneficial, 217 horse-power was still not going to get the job done against a 4.6L V8, at least not in our full-dress street Focus. We decided early on not to cheat on our project by strip-ping the car down to the bare essentials. While certainly beneficial for lowering e.t.s, we wanted to have all the perform-ance with the comfort of A/C, power windows, and cruise control. While no one will ever confuse the Focus with a 7-series BMW or S-class Mercedes, we wanted to make sure the street car name still applied to our project vehicle. After all, the project Focus was still being employed as a daily driver by the author at the time of the buildup.

With the blower already pumping out 12-13 psi of boost near redline, we chose to improve the power output without resorting to another increase in boost pressure. After all, there is a limit to what can be expected of a Roots-style supercharger. With increased rotor speed and boost pressure comes a dra-matic increase in charge temperature. Unfortunately, space constraints elimi-nated the chance of any type of inter-cooler, something certainly beneficial when boost exceeds 10 psi. This is espe-cially true of Roots superchargers, as they are notoriously inefficient at higher boost levels. The Roots blowers excel at producing immediate boost and power response, but were never intended for high-boost applications. If all worked as planned, our increase in power would come with a drop in boost. Our plan was to improve the efficiency of the motor using conventional techniques, namely revised cam timing and improved cylinder head flow. Since the boost pressure registered on your gauge is nothing more than back pressure pres-ent in the intake system, improving the efficiency of the motor would not only improve power but also help reduce some of that unwanted back pressure (boost). The resulting drop in boost should make life easier on the supercharger not to mention lowering our inlet charge temperature.

The game plan included removing the stock Zetec cylinder head and shipping it to Focus Central for porting. While removed, Focus Central also fit the head with new Crane cam profiles. The intake cam featured 210 degrees of duration at .050 while the exhaust cam measured 206 degrees. The lift specs were likewise skewed in favor of the intake, with the intake measuring .374 in. and the exhaust .366 in. The cams were ground on a 110-degree lobe separation angle. The Focus Central head

package also featured head porting, but this early example featured only intake porting. Focus Central has made great advances in head porting since this particular buildup, but the results were still impressive. Check out the 223-hp "all motor" and 500-hp turbo buildups for proof that their head porting program is now running at full steam. The stock short block remained unmodified. Equipped with the Jackson Racing M62 supercharger, ProM meter, and 36-pound injectors, the Focus Central head/cam package allowed us to reach our goal of 235 wheel horsepower, though oddly enough there was very little drop in the boost pressure. Had we elected to build this combination again, there would have been even more extensive head porting, wilder cam profiles,

and a Pectel engine management system. Additional mods to the motor (run before and after the head package) included a Focus Sport long-tube header and off-road pipe, Focus Central adjustable cam sprockets, a 65mm throttle body, Borla exhaust and Crane HI6 ignition amplifier with boost retard (not used when running race fuel).

Test 3
300-hp F-Max Turbocharged Zetec Buildup

After completing the Project ZX3-GT, the author removed the Jackson Racing supercharger and began looking for another source of motivation for the Focus. After driving the Focus in normally aspirated trim for 1,000 miles or

Test 3: 300-hp F-Max Turbocharged Zetec Buildup

Engine Specifications

Block:	Stock
Crank:	Stock
Rods:	Stock
Pistons:	Stock
Head:	Focus Central ported
Valves:	Stock
Cams:	Crane 210/206
Sprockets:	Focus Central Adjustable
Intake:	Focus Central Modified 2000 Zetec
Throttle body:	65mm
Air intake:	Custom F-Max
Filter:	Cone
Maf:	None
Header:	F-Max Turbo Manifold
Exhaust:	Borla
Injectors:	72 lbs./hr.
Turbo:	F-Max-Turbonetics
Blower:	NA
Boost level:	18-19 psi

Management:	Pectel		Intercooler:	F-Max air-to-air
Fuel pump:	Stock with Kenne Bell Boost-a-Pump		Nitrous:	No

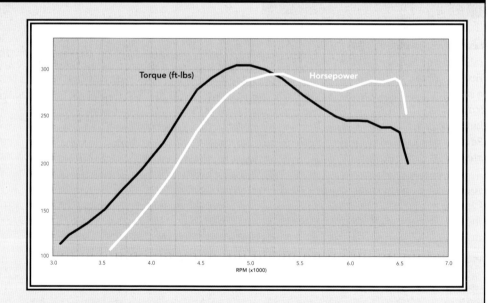

Adding a quality turbo kit like the system from F-Max to your Zetec motor can produce exceptional power. We managed to produce 300 wheel horsepower and over 300 ft-lbs of torque. Note that the horsepower peak came at 5,400 rpm, while the torque peak came at 4,900 rpm. Running just 7 psi and 192 wheel horsepower, this motor was a blast to drive on a daily basis. Running 18-19 psi, this motor was a real tire-smoking animal.

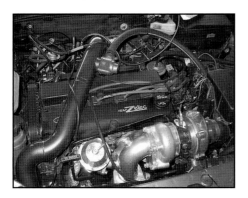

Test 3: Things really started to get serious once I installed the F-Max turbo kit on the Zetec motor. Ford really needs a turbo Focus, as this F-Max kit at just 7 psi would walk all over an SVT Focus.

Test 3: The F-Max kit relied on a Turbonetics T3-TO4B hybrid turbo to supply the necessary boost to the Focus motor. We know from experience that this turbo was good for at least 300 wheel horsepower.

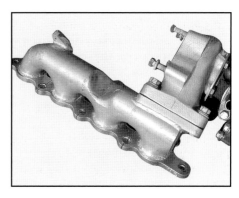

Test 3: The F-Max kit featured a log-style exhaust manifold that helped improve turbo response. The custom exhaust manifold also made installation and servicing the system quite easy.

Test 3: The F-Max kit was usually run with a set of 36 pound injectors and matching (calibrated) ProM meter, but we had to jump up to 72-pound injectors and a Pectel management system when we made 300 horsepower.

so, it was definitely time for a change. Once you have a motor with forced induction, it is hard to go back to a normally aspirated motor, even a modified

one. With over 200 wheel horsepower available in supercharged trim, Honda and Acura street cars were pretty easy game. Even all-motor LS/VTEC hybrids were no match for the supercharged motors, unless the owners had seriously stripped their cars. Dropping from over 200 wheel horsepower to well under 150 wheel horsepower felt like someone had pulled a few spark plugs. No longer could you accelerate past slower vehicles on the freeway with a simple flick of the throttle. It now took full throttle and a downshift, not to mention a ton of noise from the long-tube headers and Borla exhaust. Though the supercharged motor relied on the same exhaust, at least motivation accompanied the extra noise. Having a loud car that is also slow is really inexcusable.

The answer to my normally aspirated blues came from F-Max in the form of their Zetec turbo kit. The kit included

everything necessary to bolt on anywhere from 7-18 psi of boost (depending on turbo size). The kit included a log-style exhaust manifold, a Turbonetics turbocharger, and front-mounted air-to-air intercooler. The turbo was a T3/T04 hybrid capable of supporting up to (as

Test 3: Running at 18-19 psi on the Dyno-Jet, the author's personal Focus pumped out right at 300 wheel horsepower and 306 ft-lbs of torque.

Test 3: Though probably overkill at just 7 psi, the F-Max kit included a front-mounted air-to-air intercooler.

Test 3: The stock fuel pump was good for about 250 wheel hp, but we coaxed 300 hp using this Kenne Bell Boost-a-Pump.

Test 3: The turbo boost was controlled using this Turbo XS manual waste gate controller.

we found out) 300 wheel horsepower. The air-to-air intercooler bolted right in place and dropped the charge temps down by a good 150 degrees (at 268 degree inlet). At lower (street) boost levels, the intercooler was probably not even necessary, as the charge temperature exiting the turbo was pretty low at just 7 psi. The kit also included the necessary plumbing to connect the turbo to the intercooler and the intercooler to the throttle body. Naturally F-Max included an inlet system to mount the mass air meter. Surprisingly enough, the small cone filter used in the kit flowed more than enough to support 300 horsepower (it was tested against another larger filter). A compressor bypass valve and waste gate were included as well.

This early F-max kit did not include any form of fuel or timing management. In fact, this kit was used to develop the management systems. As the F-max kit came along after the Jackson Racing supercharger buildup, the Zetec motor was already equipped with both a Crane HI6 ignition system (with timing retard) and a ProM meter and RC injector combination. The ProM mass air meter was calibrated for the larger 36 lbs./hr. injectors from RC Engineering. The timing retard function offered by the Crane ignition was not employed with the boost set at 7 psi (on pump gas), but was occasionally used with elevated boost levels. The 36-pound injectors and ProM meter were eventually swapped for a set of larger 72-pound (converted 36 pound Ford injectors—PowerTrain Dynamics (714) 373-0068 injectors and Pectel stand-alone engine management system. The 36-pound injectors were simply not large enough to supply the fuel needs of the F-Max motor once the boost was run past 13-14 psi. It was also necessary to install a Kenne Bell Boost-a-Pump to increase the fuel flow of the stock fuel pump. The stock Focus pump will not support 300 wheel horsepower.

The motor was equipped just as it had been with the supercharger, save for installing a Focus Central intake manifold. The 2000 Zetec intake featured porting and epoxy to improve the flow rate by some 25 cfm per runner. The result was an intake worth a solid 10-12

horsepower (see intake chapter) over the stock manifold without sacrificing any low-speed torque. Naturally the long-tube header was replaced by the turbo manifold, but the off-road down pipe and flex pipe were retained, as was the Borla cat-back exhaust. We employed a Turbo XS waste gate controller to adjust the boost pressure. Nathan Tasukon was on hand from Pectel to program the engine management system. After a few key strokes, Nathan had the turbo Zetec motor up and running with the larger injectors. After some tuning, the modified Zetec motor produced 296 wheel horsepower and 306 ft-lbs of torque using the F-Max turbo kit. Attempts to up the boost pressure resulted in little or no power gain. It is possible that more power can be had from the F-Max kit, it would simply take a larger turbo. As it is, the F-Max kit provided thousands of trouble-free turbocharged miles, and more than a dozen torqued-off Honda/Acura owners who lost when they paired up against it at a stoplight!

Test 4
12-Second, 223-hp, All-Motor Focus Central Zetec

At the time of this writing, there were no 12-second "all motor" Foci to be found. Heck, running a 12-second Zetec motor with nitrous or some form of forced induction was pretty impressive. Witness the 13-second Jackson Racing supercharged buildup listed elsewhere in this chapter. The importance of

a 12-second all-motor Zetec might be hard to grasp given the number of 12-second all-motor Hondas running around, but remember back when VTEC Hondas were in their infancy? Heck, think about how many non-VTEC all-motor Hondas are out running 12s. That kind of puts things into a better perspective. Whether the fast Focus can be made to run head to head with the hellacious Hondas of the world remains to be seen, but one thing's for sure, there is plenty of power waiting to be unleashed inside the stock Zetec motor. Witness the latest time slip of the Focus Central "all motor" assault. Run at 2,430 pounds, the Focus has managed a best drag strip time of 12.96 at 105.4 miles per hour. Imagine, even with the rather portly weight (race Hondas go just 1,600-1,700 pounds), the Focus Central Focus has gone where no Focus has gone before. Chances are good that a great many will follow (possible even before this book goes to print), but always remember who got there first.

The 12-second run has brought much more than an impressive ET and elevated trap speed. The age-old adage of race on Sunday and sell on Monday was applied at Focus Central. The testing that went into the buildup brought with it a wealth of information about particular engine combinations. Along the way, it squashed any notion that the stock Zetec short blocks are anything but stout. Early on, the powdered metal rods developed a reputation for being weak (don't ya just love the internet?). Those

Test 4: Under that custom air filter assembly is a 223-hp all-motor (stock short block) 2.0L Zetec motor capable of pushing a Focus into the 12s.

Test 4: Though equipped with the stock short block, the Zetec featured a host of modifications including custom Crower cams and adjustable cam sprockets.

Test 4: 12-Second , 223-hp
All-Motor Focus Central Zetec

Engine Specifications

Block:	Stock Zetec
Crank:	Stock Zetec
Rods:	Stock Zetec
Pistons:	Stock Zetec
Head:	Focus Central ported & milled (.070)
Valves:	1mm oversize
Cams:	Crower Stage 4+
Sprockets:	Focus Central Adjustable
Intake:	Custom Dual Throttle Body
Throttle body(s):	Dual Focus Central 65mm
Air intake:	Custom
Filter:	None
Maf:	None
Header:	Focus Central 1 3/4-inch Race
Exhaust:	Focus central 2.5-inch
Injectors:	30 lbs./hr.

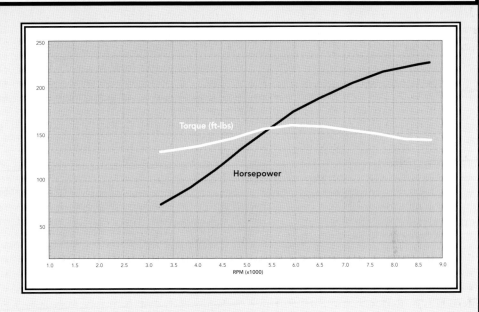

Running nothing more than a stock short block, the gang at Focus Central managed to produce 223 hp and nearly 160 ft-lbs of torque.

Turbo:	NA	Fuel pump:	Stock
Blower:	NA	Intercooler:	NA
Boost level:	NA	Nitrous:	No
Management:	Pectel Stand Alone		

unfortunate few who experienced problems with the reciprocating assembly were obviously owner-induced. Need proof? Witness the numerous 8,200-rpm shifts at the track, combined with as much as a few hundred dyno runs exceeding 8,000 rpm and you can see that the stock Zetec reciprocating assembly is all too happy to run some 1,300-rpm past the factory redline. Focus Central is quick to point out that the 8,000-rpm running can only be accomplished with proper tuning, meaning safe air/fuel and timing curves. No motor, regardless of origin, will stand up to detonation for any length of time.

While an 8,000-rpm motor is nice, it doesn't guarantee 12-second time slips. A 12-second Focus needs one thing—horsepower. A stock 130-hp 2.0L Zetec motor will produce anywhere from 105 hp-109 hp at the wheels on a DynoJet. Propelling a 2,460-pound Focus into the

12s required doubling the factory power output. Doubling the factory power output required plenty of airflow. The high-RPM Zetec short block allowed Focus Central to shift the torque curve sufficiently to produce the desired high-RPM horsepower. An example works well here regarding the correlation between horsepower and torque production. A stock 2.0L Zetec will produce roughly 109 horsepower at 5,500 rpm. Ford purposely designed the power curve to be torquey. The torquey nature traded throttle response and low-speed power production for top-end horsepower. At the power peak of 5,500 rpm, the stock Zetec's power output of 109 hp equates to 104 ft-lbs of torque (at the wheels). If we calculate the power production using the same torque figure at 8,000 rpm using the formula $Hp = Tq \times rpm / 5{,}252$, we see that 104 ft-lbs produced at 8,000 rpm will give us 158

horsepower. By shifting the torque curve 2,500 rpm, we have gained nearly 50 horsepower.

It is true that producing the same torque value at a higher RPM would bring extra horsepower, but the shift alone won't produce sufficient power to put a Focus into the 12s. In order to coax 220+ horsepower out of the 2.0L Zetec motor, the gang at Focus Central had to concentrate on stuffing more airflow through the motor. They attacked the airflow problem from a variety of different angles, including head porting, cam timing, and free-flowing exhaust. For good measure, they included some additional compression, a trick dual-throttle body intake and clever mapping thanks to a stand-alone fuel injection. It wasn't long before the test motor breached the 200-hp mark. Naturally when you talk about airflow, the first thing to come up is the cylinder head.

Test 4: One of the many trick items of the race motor was this dual-throttle body intake manifold.

Test 4: A larger-tube race header was also employed on the 12-second machine.

Test 4: The head was given the full porting treatment, which improved the flow by as much as 40 cfm per runner.

According to Dennis Hilliard, the stock 2.0L Zetec head flowed pretty marginal out of the box. The intake port struggled to break 200 cfm at .450 valve lift while the exhaust trailed by some 40 cfm. After extensive time on the flow bench, the intake port topped 255 cfm at .450 lift, while the exhaust was up to 199 cfm at the same valve lift. Additional modifications to the head included 1mm oversized valves. The head was also milled .070 to increase the compression ratio by nearly a full point. For a point of reference, the Focus Central ported Zetec head easily out-flowed a B-series VTEC Honda head.

Next on the list were the cam timing and intake manifold. Extensive testing revealed that the modified Zetec motor responded well to aggressive cam timing. Dennis Hilliard from Focus Central

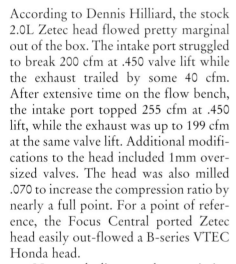

Test 4: This custom aluminum race clutch became necessary once the rev limit was removed. Shifting at 8200 rpm literally exploded stock and modified clutches. This DPG clutch is available exclusively from Focus Central.

eventually settled on a pair of custom Stage 4 cams from Crower. Don't for a minute think that the cams were a one-shot deal. The "stock block" race motor has gone through at least a dozen or so different cam profiles before finding a pair to allow the motor to exceed 220 horsepower. Given the intake to exhaust flow relationship on the ported head, single-pattern or even dual-pattern cams favoring the intake seemed to be the way to go. At this power level, only hours and hours of testing can determine what cam specs will work with a given combination. Knowing that the wilder cam profiles were going to want to make peak power well beyond 5,500 rpm, the guys at Focus Central designed a short-runner intake manifold to allow the motor to take full advantage of the aggressive cam timing. (Check out the intake chapter for the long and short of intake design). When it comes to intake manifolds, long runners (like the factory manifold) produce plenty of low-speed torque. Unfortunately, this design suffers at high RPM. Short runners are tuned to trade some low-speed torque for exceptional high-RPM power. Not wanting to restrict the short-runner composite intake, Focus Central decided to drill the manifold to accept a pair of their billet 65mm throttle bodies.

Airflow that is introduced into the motor must eventually find its way out. What began in the ported exhaust port of the Focus Central modified cylinder head continued into a 11/4-inch long-tube, 4 into 1 race header. As with the cam timing and intake manifold, the race

header design works best with the wilder engine combination. Focus Central also offers a slightly smaller-tube (Tri-Y) version for milder motors as well as a set of shorty replacement headers. Like most things in life, when it comes to headers, one size most definitely does not fit all. Headers work much like intake manifolds in that the primary diameter (and length) work with the cam timing to maximize exhaust scavenging. It is this scavenging that improves the power output. Naturally, this scavenging must be tuned for a given application. The race header works best at elevated engine speeds (on the race motor), but would not likely perform as well on a mild Zetec motor. To complete the exhaust flow, Focus Central installed a 2.5-inch cat-back exhaust, flex pipe, and off-road down pipe

Though the headliners are the most important, Focus Central did not forget the rest of the supporting cast. Given the

Test 4: The 12-second red rocket sported a carbon fiber hood with functional hood scoop, a set of lightweight Wilwood brakes, and a trick coil-over suspension.

milled cylinder head and wild cam timing, it seems only natural that Focus Central installed a set of their adjustable cam sprockets to fine-tune to power curve. According to Dennis Hilliard, their adjustable sprockets were worth as much as 10-12 horsepower at various points along the curve. Dennis was just as quick to credit the Pectel engine management system for allowing him to optimize the wild all-motor combination. Designed as a near plug-n-play system for the Focus, the Pectel eliminated the mass air meter from the management equation and allowed Focus Central to tune the air/fuel and timing curves on the wild 8,000-rpm Zetec. As expected, the tuning took some time, but eventually the Focus Central crew got a handle on the new system and big power numbers began to show on the

dyno. The numbers were large enough that the new motor required 30-pound injectors in place of the factory squirters. When things were all said and done, the 2.0L "All Motor" Zetec pumped out 223 wheel horsepower at 8,400 rpm and 159 ft-lbs of torque at 5,600 rpm. Note that the torque peak was now where the horsepower used to be on the stock motor.

Test 5
514-hp Innovative Turbocharged Zetec Buildup

After running my mildly modified Zetec motor with the F-Max turbo kit (see 300-hp buildup elsewhere in this chapter), I took a trip to Ken Duttweiler's place to do a story on the turbo system he was running on his Focus.

The system differed from the F-Max kit in that instead of the log-style exhaust manifold, the Duttweiler/Innovative turbo system utilized a tubular header to feed the turbo. The header was a real stainless steel work of art (see header photo). It seemed obvious that the header should provide more power than a simple log-style exhaust manifold, but how would the two compare when it comes to turbo response or longevity? Unfortunately, I did not get a chance to test the longevity of either the F-max (log-style) or Innovative (header) systems, as the two were installed for no more than 7000-8000 miles. Both were driven daily on the street, as the Innovative system eventually employed on the 500-hp buildup was used previously on the same modified motor run with the F-max kit. Thanks to a larger Innovative

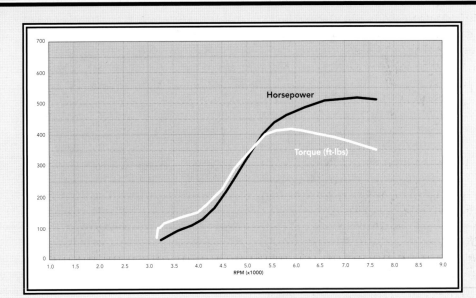

Test 5: 514-hp Innovative Turbocharged Zetec Buildup

Engine Specifications

Block:	Stock
Crank:	Stock
Rods:	Crower
Pistons:	Sean Hyland/JE
Head:	Focus Central (extensively ported)
Valves:	1mm oversize
Cams:	Custom Crower
Sprockets:	Focus Central
Intake:	Ford Racing
Throttle body:	65mm
Air intake:	4-inch Custom
Filter:	4x12-inch K&N
Maf:	None
Header:	Innovative Tubular
Exhaust:	Borla
Injectors:	72 lbs./hr.
Turbo:	Innovative GT66
Blower:	NA
Boost level:	29 psi
Management:	Pectel

It didn't happen without a lot of hard work, but this modified 2.0L Focus motor managed to produce 514 wheel horsepower and 415 ft-lbs of torque. Credit the Innovative header and GT66 turbo along with the Pectel management system and Sean Hyland short block.

Fuel pump:	Aeromotive with custom return fuel system (Kenne Bell Boost-a-Pump)	Intercooler:	Vortech air-to-water Aftercooler
		Nitrous:	No

Test 5: The 514-hp buildup started with a Sean Hyland short block that featured forged 9.1:1 pistons.

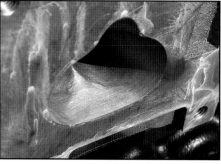

Test 5: Focus Central performed their magic on the cylinder head, greatly improving the intake and exhaust flow.

Test 5: The Innovative Turbo system included a stainless steel tubular exhaust header to mount the turbo.

turbo (T04E-46), the Zetec motor produced 365 wheel horsepower with the Innovative kit. The larger GT66 turbo was reserved for the dedicated turbo motor equipped with forged rods and pistons, as I had every intention of boosting it to within an inch of its life.

After running the Innovative turbo kit on the modified Zetec motor (to the tune of 365 wheel horsepower), it was removed and set aside in preparation for the "big motor." The big motor was actually no bigger than the small motor, but the designation referred to the big horsepower we hoped to produce. The short block was supplied by Sean Hyland Motorsports and consisted of a stock Zetec block and crank, but with forged rods and pistons. I have previously extolled the virtues of the strength of the stock reciprocating assembly, but nearly quadrupling the stock power output goes above and beyond the expectations of any stock short block. The forged rods and pistons were deemed absolutely nec-

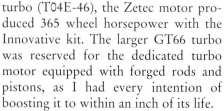

Test 5: The stock block and crank were retained, but the short block also included forged rods for additional strength at high RPM and boost levels.

essary to allow us to run the combination of power level and engine speed we had planned for the turbo motor. The static compression of the forged Zetec motor worked out to just over 9.0:1 with a stock (unmilled) cylinder head.

Speaking of cylinder head, every effort was made to increase the power output of the normally aspirated combination, including extensive porting. The reason for paying such close attention to the normally aspirated power output is that the NA power gains are multiplied by the pressure ratio once you add boost to the equation. Suppose you have a 100 horsepower (NA) motor and your goal is to produce 300 horsepower with a turbo. A normally aspirated motor actually has 14.7 psi of (atmospheric) pressure filling the cylinders. This is referred to as 1 bar. If your motor makes 100 horsepower at atmospheric pressure, doubling the pressure (2 bar or 14.7 psi on top of the atmospheric pressure already present) will likely double the output to 200 hp. Upping it further to 300 hp will require another bar or 14.7 psi, bringing the total to 29.4 psi. If you increased the power output of the normally aspirated motor to 150 hp (using ported head, cams, and/or intake), making 300 horsepower would only require 14.7 psi, since 2 times 150 hp equals 300 hp. While turbocharged motors don't always cooperate this readily, sometimes it is possible to more than double the power output at 14.7 psi. Regardless of the eventual output, the better the NA motor, the better the turbo motor.

Knowing this, I decided that the best course was to build an efficient nor-

mally aspirated Zetec motor before pumping it full of boost. The goal was 500 wheel horsepower, but I would be happy with anything over 450 wheel horsepower. A 109-hp stock Zetec motor would require over 52 psi to produce the desired power output (if it would ever get there). I hoped to up the NA power closer to 200 wheel horsepower to allow the 500-hp number to be achieved using somewhere between 20-24 psi. We had run 24 psi on the mild Zetec combination with good results and knew that the GT66 was plenty capable of supporting 500+hp at 25+ psi, so everything looked good to go. The head was given to Focus Central for extensive porting. The porting matched the work applied to their 12-second all-motor effort (not surprising since this turbo motor was destined to power a Focus Central drag race machine). The head flow was increased by 40 cfm on the intake side and 32 cfm on the exhaust. Custom Crower cams were chosen based on the intake-to-exhaust flow relationship. The cams offered 246 degrees of intake duration with .448 lift and 244 degrees of exhaust duration with .440 lift. Naturally Focus Central cam sprockets were also installed. Tuning the cams produced plenty of additional power (see chapter on cams and cam sprockets).

With the head and cams taken care of, Focus Central supplied a custom intake manifold. Remember what we mentioned about shifting the torque curve (see 12-second buildup elsewhere in this chapter)? Producing 500 horsepower at just 6,000 rpm would require

438 ft-lbs of torque. Doing the same thing at 7,500 rpm would only require the production of 350 ft-lbs. The short-runner intake effectively shifted the power curve higher in the rev range. Though the composite Focus Central intake worked well, we produced the best power using the Ford Racing cast aluminum intake (modified by Focus Central to properly fit). The longer runners in the Ford Racing intake improved turbo response and bolstered the torque curve compared to the short-runner composite intake from Focus Central. In addition to the runner length, the two intakes differed in the position of the throttle body. The Focus Central composite intake repositioned the throttle body near the stock SVT position (low and adjacent to cylinder four). The Ford Racing intake positioned the 65mm throttle body in the stock location.

Naturally the highlight of the 514-hp turbo buildup was the turbo system. Supplied by Innovative Turbo, the system mirrored the one used by Ken Duttweiller. In fact, it was the testing on the Ken Duttweiller turbo Focus that prompted this 514-hp buildup. The Innovative Turbo "kit" consisted of a tubular stainless steel header and custom GT66 turbo. The GT66 turbo was capable of supporting in excess of 600 horsepower, so we knew it would be more than sufficient for our needs. The header was a work of art, not to mention being much easier to install than the factory exhaust. Unlike the F-Max kit (much

more of a complete kit) the Innovative Turbo header positioned the turbo away from the cylinder head and above the transmission. This position allowed the turbo to take advantage of the pulse tuning offered by the long-tube header design. The header also featured a provision for the external (Innovative) waste gate. Positioning of the waste gate relative to the direction of exhaust flow is critical to effective operation. The waste gate tube should be lined up with the exhaust flow to maximize the response rate and effectiveness. This system was configured to dump the exhaust from the waste gate to the atmosphere.

The final performance component came in the form of an air-to-water intercooler system supplied by Vortech Engineering (the supercharger people). The After Cooler core was originally designed to run on a supercharged Civic Si, but was ushered into Focus duty by the author. A custom inlet tube was fabricated (by the author) to use with the Innovative GT66, the Vortech After-cooler, and the 65mm throttle body. The Innovative waste gate was controlled by an APEXi electronic waste gate controller. The fuel and timing curves were controlled by a Pectel stand-alone engine management system and 72-pound per hour injectors. The injectors were fed using an Aeromotive high-pressure pump capable of supporting in excess of 1,000 hp, even without the Kenne Bell Boost-a-Pump. A return style fuel system was built for the 500-

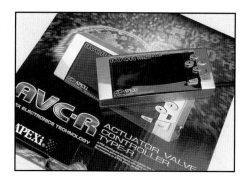

Test 5: Rather than rely on a simple manual waste gate controller, we got sophisticated on this buildup and installed an APEXi Super AVC Type R controller. The APEXi system functioned perfectly and allowed us to pump up the boost pressure to 29 psi.

hp motor, including a custom fuel rail (modified stock with fittings), an adjustable fuel pressure regulator, and 118-octane (no detonation) Union 76 race fuel. It took a couple of late nights at the Sho Shop (thanks to Vadim, Dave and Josh for their help) tuning the combination, but after cranking up the boost (using the APEXi Super AVC), we (mostly Nathan Tasukon from Pectel) finally got the combination to pump out 514 hp and 412 ft-lbs of torque at 29 psi of boost. There was more power to be had from the combination, but we ran out of adjustment on the APEXi Super AVC and we were nearly maxed out on the injectors. The turbo motor is scheduled to make passes in a Focus Central drag race Focus in the very near future.

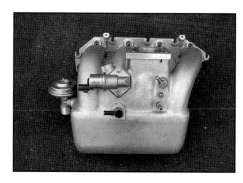

Test 5: A number of manifolds were tried on the turbo motor, but we eventually exceeded 500 wheel horsepower with the unit from Ford Racing. The manifold required some modifications before it could be installed on the Zetec motor.

Test 5: The heart of the system from Innovative was the GT66 turbo. According to the compressor map, the GT66 turbo was capable of supporting well over 600 horsepower, or more than enough to meet our goals.

Test 5: Crower supplied a pair of custom cams that allowed us to take full advantage of the improved cylinder head flow. The cams offered 246 degrees of intake duration with .448 lift and 244 degrees of exhaust duration with .440 lift.

DROPPED & STOPPED

CANYON CARVERS AND BETTER BINDERS

For most enthusiasts, the word performance means horsepower. In reality, performance or better yet high performance can come in many forms. The engine compartment of your Zetec or SVT isn't the only place on your Focus that needs attention. The suspension, brakes and even the transmission can be improved upon. This chapter covers some of the possible upgrades available for both the Zetec and SVT versions with regards to suspension, brakes, and even drive train. Swapping out the stock suspension for a complete adjustable coil-over system can transform your mundane little grocery getter into a

canyon carver of the highest magnitude. Looking for something a little less radical, with more street manners? We have included an installation of a Sean Hyland Dynamic suspension system. With all that horsepower and handling, shouldn't your Focus be blessed with brakes to match? Focus Central has a rear disc brake kit that utilizes all factory Ford components. How about that clutch, think it will hold up to a full-throttle launch under boost? The final section of this chapter deals with installing a Ford Racing limited slip diff, Aasco aluminum flywheel, and Power Tone high-performance clutch. By no

means all encompassing, the sections should at least provide information to help you make an informed decision.

Hyland's Dynamic Suspension

When it comes time to choose suspension components, especially if your plan of attack includes a complete makeover, the systems approach is a tried and true method.

While it is possible to piece together all of the usual suspension components (shocks, springs, and sway bars) from different sources, the end result can be a conglomeration of mismatched components. For optimum performance, the components must all work in harmony, especially if ride quality made your suspension goals list. There is nothing worse than installing all of the trick new suspension components on your Focus only to have the car bounce and wander all over the road. While it is true that some of the best handling front-wheel drive vehicles on the planet (British Touring Cars) rely on ultra-high spring rates and the attending shock valving, there is a dramatic difference between a British Touring Car and your typical street Focus. You'll not find many Touring Cars next to you on the freeway during the daily commute, nor will you find them traversing the series of potholes that frequent the frontage roads

The engine compartment isn't the only place to find additional performance. The right suspension and brakes will allow you to take full advantage of all that new-found horsepower.

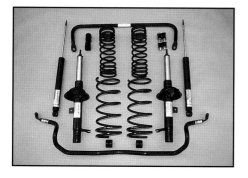

The Dynamic suspension from Sean Hyland Motorsports came with everything we needed to transform the ZX3 into a first-class handler.

It's all about cornering.

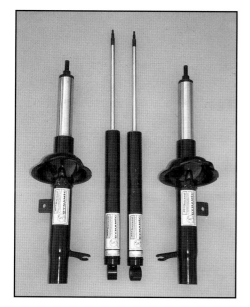

One of the critical elements in the new suspension was this quartet of Dynamic Suspension shocks and struts. Sean Hyland did extensive testing to come up with the proper shock valving for the Focus.

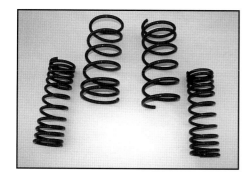

The revised valving worked in conjunction with the new spring rates. We installed both front and rear coil springs to both lower the car and improve handling.

and side streets used to get home. The same can be said for steep driveways, freeway expansion strips and the occasional dirt road.

While ultimate handling and ride quality are certainly at odds, the proper combination of components can produce elevated levels of handling and performance without resulting to a bone-jarring ride. True, you're not likely to overtake Alain Menu on the outside of turn 3, but you will likely retain use of your kidneys and pancreas for many years to come. That's got to be worth something. As mentioned earlier, the key to maximizing cornering power without beating your internals to death with excessive spring rate and shock valving is to install a complete suspension system that has been thoroughly tested and refined. Naturally such a system is difficult (if not impossible) to find in the aftermarket. Ford spent untold hours fine tuning the ride quality on the Focus, ditto for the engineers at SVT, but such expenditures would overwhelm most aftermarket companies. Many suspension systems are the result of piece-mealing together available components. The problem with this approach is that the available spring rates may not be optimized for the available shock valving. The (possible)

exception to this rule is a coil-over system (like the systems installed elsewhere in this chapter). A true coil-over system allows easy changes in spring rate to match the available shock valving.

The system installed on the author's 2001 Focus came from Sean Hyland Motorsports. The system was chosen for two main reasons, the first of which was that the Focus was to be first and foremost a street car, one that would be used as daily transportation. While improved handling was expected (and important), the ultimate grip took a back seat to ride quality. Not every Focus owner is willing to pay the price for that little bit of extra grip. If track times were the ultimate yard stick, the suspension system choices may be different, but for a street car or even a double duty machine (occasionally running open track events or a weekend autocross), the Sean Hyland system seemed to be the ideal choice. Reason number two for choosing the Sean Hyland components is that they were tested and shipped as a complete system. Unlike many so-called suspension experts, Sean Hyland performs extensive street and track testing, even going so far as to test a number of different tire combinations with the shock/spring/bar package. As a national champion road racer, I understand what it takes to get a

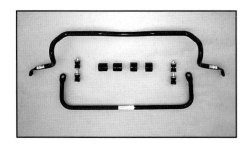

These front and rear sway bars were slightly larger than stock. They were used to minimize the extensive body roll present in the stock ZX3 suspension. Naturally the bars came with urethane bushings to further improve their response rate.

The first step was to jack up the rear of the car and remove the rear sway bar. Here the factory end link was being unbolted.

After positioning a jack under the lower arm, we unbolted the spindle.

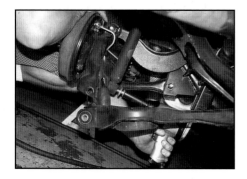

Next came the lower shock mounting bolt.

car to handle. That understanding breeds appreciation for the effort put into combining improved handling with excellent street manners, as achieving one or the other is difficult enough. Combining both is quite extraordinary.

The Dynamic Suspension from Sean Hyland seemed to fit the bill perfectly for the street Focus. The complete system included all of the usual components in the quest for improved performance. Hyland's package included performance struts (& rear shocks), springs, and sway bars. In addition to the hard parts, Sean Hyland also supplied a set of 17x7 wheels shod with a quartet of BFG G-Force TA KDW tires. According to Hyland, no less than 5 different tire combinations were tested before choosing the G-Force KDWs. Having now driven the Focus with the Dynamic suspension, I'd say they made the right choice. The G-Force TAs offer exceptional grip for a street tire. The TAs came mounted on 5-spoke alloy wheels. Though larger than the factory offerings, the change in appearance offered by the Sean Hyland wheels was subtle. Subtle is perhaps the best way to describe the entire suspension. No slammed or dumped in the weeds look here. If that is your bag, look elsewhere for a set of cut springs. If you want useable performance, the Sean Hyland system might be just the ticket.

As always, the first step in installing the Dynamic suspension was to remove the factory bits. Starting out back, we removed the factory rear sway bar. The rear was secured by four mounting bolts and a pair of end links. We removed the factory end links as Sean supplied a set of urethane end links along with matching mount bushings. Once the rear bar was removed, we turned our attention to the remainder of the rear suspension. The next step was to unbolt the spindle from the lower arm, but only after positioning a jack under the control arm. Lowering the jack eliminated the spring tension allowing us to remove the rear coil spring. Removing the rear shock was just as easy, requiring only two mounting bolts. It was necessary to remove two interior panels to allow access to the upper rear shock bolt. It was also neces-

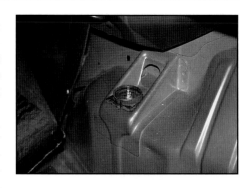

Access to the upper bolt required removal of a few interior body panels.

Here is the stock rear shock next to the new Dynamic Suspension supplied by Sean Hyland. The new shock was a direct bolt in.

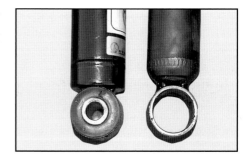

Before we could install the new shock, we had to swap over the lower mount bushing. The old bushing was first pressed out of the old shock and then pressed back into the new shock.

Check out the difference between the factory ZX3 spring and the Sean Hyland unit. The new spring was both lower and stiffer to improve handling.

The front strut assembly was unbolted and removed from the front spindle. Note the front sway bar has already been replaced.

sary to hold the tip of the shock shaft (to stop it from spinning) while unbolting the retaining nut. With the rear shocks removed, we had the entire stock rear suspension out and were ready to install the Sean Hyland components.

Before installing the Dynamic suspension rear shocks, it was necessary to transfer the stock shock bushings. We pressed out the stock lower mount bushings (see rear shock photo). This was accomplished using a vice and a two-jaw puller (the kind available at most auto part stores). The vice was employed to press the bushings into the

eyelet of the new shocks. We also swapped over the stock bump rubbers, upper sleeves and top mounts onto the new shocks. As expected of a systems-approach suspension, all of the Sean Hyland components went in without a hitch. The shocks came first, followed by the new lowering springs and then the larger rear sway bar. We made sure to reuse the stock upper spring cup when installing the new springs. The floor jack was used to position the lower control arm back in place to allow us to bolt the new suspension together. After mounting the rear sway bar (using new urethane mount bushings in the factory mounts), we installed the new (urethane) end links. The urethane components help reduce unwanted deflection in the bushings, something that improves the response rate of the sway bar. Less body roll means better handling. Once we had everything tight, we installed the trick, new 17-inch Sean Hyland/BFG wheel and tire package.

With the rear components installed, we turned our attention to the front suspension. Unlike the rear, the front suspension consisted of a strut/spring assembly. Removal of the front assembly was a four-bolt affair. The top three mounting bolts were removed followed by a single lower retaining bolt clamping the strut. On the passenger's side, it was necessary to pry down on the lower control arm to facilitate removal of the strut/spring assembly, but the driver's side required no such assistance. With both front struts removed, we attacked the front sway bar. Removal of the front sway bar required removing the end links, four mounting bolts and then removal of the exhaust down pipe. This last item really made life much easier when it came time to pull the twisted sway bar out one side. The Sean Hyland bar installed in reverse order. Naturally we included the supplied urethane mount bushings. Removal of the stock springs and installation of the Sean Hyland springs (on the Dynamic struts) required a coil-spring compressor (thanks for the help Sho Shop). The entire assembly went on as one unit and we buttoned everything up including the trick factory front sway bar end

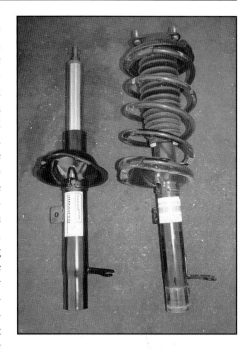

After removal of the single lower mounting bolt, we removed the front spring/strut assembly. It is shown here next to the Sean Hyland Dynamic Suspension front strut. Note the extra thick shaft on the Sean Hyland unit.

A spring compressor was used to disassemble the front struts. The Sean Hyland components were assembled using the factory upper bearing plate and dust cover.

The most visual aspect of the new suspension was the wheel/tire package. The 17x7-inch 5-spoke Sean Hyland wheels shod with BFG G-Force TAs offered both visual horsepower and improved grip. The G-Force tires were an excellent choice for the Focus. The tires have over 10,000 miles on them and show very little wear.

Before beginning, we measured the stock ride height to determine how much the Sean Hyland setup would lower the car. We were looking for just over 1 inch to keep a reasonable amount of ground clearance.

links. One nice touch was that the Sean Hyland strut housings were duplicates of the factory in that they had provisions for all the factory hardware such as end links, ABS wiring, and brake lines.

After installing the remaining two 17-inch wheels on the front (remember—they are directional!), we were off for some back road testing. We took the car to a photogenic frontage road, where (as luck would have it) we could sample the newfound handling powers of the Sean Hyland suspension. Though not a track, the famous Ortega Highway in Southern California offered just about every possible combination of turns, from slow-speed off-camber, to high-speed sweepers. Even the blind turns could be taken with confidence as the Hyland-enhanced Focus simply went where it was pointed. The new suspension offered impressive levels of handling. The most noticeable change was a dramatic reduction in body roll. The stock ZX3 suspension actually offered surprisingly good turn in, the Hyland-modified machine was even better. The problem with the stock suspension was that after a decent turn in, the body would wallow over in protest. The limits were relatively high, the body just let you know that you were requesting some fancy maneuvering. Body roll with the Sean Hyland suspension was all but absent. After a responsive turn in, the body just kept its composure and hunkered down in anticipation of the next command.

The key to any good suspension is how it handles transitional situations where you motor through one left-hand turn to a right hander (often called esses). Ask the stock suspension to transition from one turn to the next and body roll was magnified (with its attending negative effect on grip). This transition is where the work done by the gang over at Sean Hyland came into play, and where most piece-meal suspensions lose their composure. Only a matched set of shock(strut) valving and spring rates will keep the car composed through a transitional series of turns. The shocks and springs must work in harmony to provide optimum grip over a wide variety of driving situations. The harmony can be felt even while cruising, as the ride quality is firmer than stock without being unduly harsh. Lots of spring rate and excessive shock valving greatly reduce ride quality. A mismatched set up can also cause porpoising (where the front

The new Dynamic suspension dropped the car approximately 1.2 inches. Now the Focus was ready for some serious canyon carving.

and back of the car oscillate up and down in sequence) on uneven road surfaces. The Sean Hyland suspension felt like a factory suspension, only more so. The Focus handled pot holes, expansion strips and even speeds bumps with nary a complaint. The new suspension felt like a complete system rather than something we pieced together, which is just what we were looking for.

Attitude Adjustment: Focus Central Coil-Over Suspension

For serious performance enthusiasts, there is no better suspension than a well-designed coil-over system. As the name implies, a coil-over system features an integrated shock (or strut), and coil spring assembly. While your run-of-the-mill MacPherson strut incorporates a strut and spring, the coil-over assembly

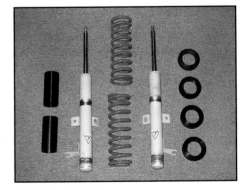

The complete system installed by Focus Central included Koni adjustable struts and shocks and coil-over adjustable sleeves and springs.

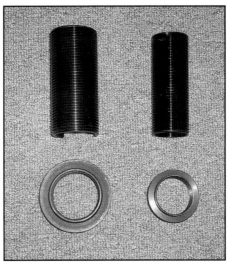

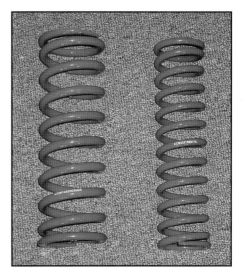

The stock ZX3 struts are hardly conducive to optimum handling.

These threaded sleeves were used to allow ride-height adjustment. By raising and/or lowering where the spring sits relative to the strut or shock, the ride can be raised or lowered.

Naturally the proper springs are necessary for use with the coil over system. These coil-over springs are available in a wide variety of different free lengths and spring rates.

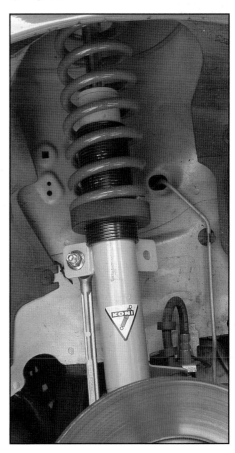

The Focus Central coil-over suspension system can be used with the stock strut, but it will be necessary to machine off the spring perch (this operation was performed to the Konis used for installation as well).

takes the combination a step further. Unlike a standard MacPherson strut assembly, a coil-over system is adjustable for ride height and generally uses a much smaller spring diameter. The coil-over assembly is adjustable thanks to a threaded sleeve and spring collar (perch). The coil spring rides on the collar, which in turn threads onto the threaded sleeve. The sleeve slides over the strut and locates (usually) on the strut mount. The ride height can be adjusted by spinning the collar on the threaded sleeve. Adjusting the collar position will raise and lower the spring and therefore the ride

Here is the front Koni coil-over strut assembly ready for installation.

Unbolting the stock strut and replacing it with the new coil-over assembly is pretty straightforward. Using the threaded sleeve, it is now possible to adjust the desired ride height.

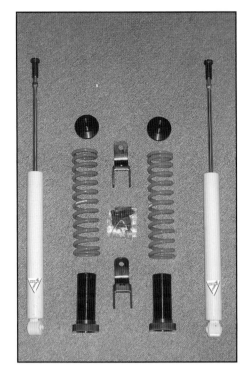

The rear coil-over system also featured Koni shocks, threaded sleeves and an adjustment collar.

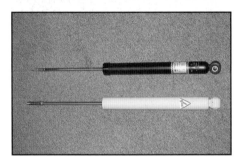

Focus Central also offers the coil-over system with Eibach shocks. The Eibach shocks are non-adjustable, so make sure to utilize the spring rates recommended by Focus Central for your application.

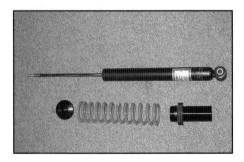

Here is the coil-over assembly in order and ready to install on the Eibach rear shock.

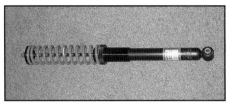

The assembled coil-over shock can now be installed on the vehicle.

The Koni rear shocks required a slightly larger spring diameter, but the assembled system is now ready for ride-height and shock valving adjustments.

The stock stamped steel Focus control arms are both heavy and non-adjustable.

Using the coil-over assembly, it is possible to adjust the ride height to your liking.

While installing the coil-over assembly on the ZX3, Focus Central also installed their tubular front and rear control arms. Note the rear control arms had previsions for a rear sway bar. Focus Central also sells drag race arms that lack the sway bar attachment points.

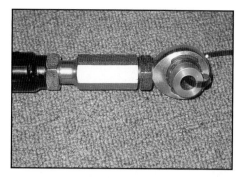

Both front and rear control arms featured beefy rod ends for added strength and to minimize deflection.

height of the vehicle. When you combine this adjustability with Koni adjustable shocks (and struts) as well as the ability to use a number of different spring rates, the coil-over system can be tailored to produce impressive handling. The system depicted here came from Focus Central and featured Koni adjustable shocks, Focus Central adjustable sleeves, and specific rate coil springs. Naturally, the coil spring rates were chosen to work in conjunction with the shock valving offered by the Konis.

The Focus Central rear control arm kit included shorter replacement arms for the rear.

Putting the "S" in SVT: Installing Coil-Over Suspension

Just like the system offered for the standard Zetec Focus, the SVT version offered full ride-height adjustment plus adjustable shock (strut) dampening. This particular coil-over assembly came from Ground Control and differed slightly from the Focus Central system installed on the standard Zetec Focus. The major difference was in the rear, where the Ground Control system produced adjustable ride height not by combining the shock with a threaded collar, but rather by separating the spring and shock. In stock form, the factory suspension featured a rear shock and separate rear coil spring. Naturally neither of the two was adjustable. Typical coil-over assemblies combine the two by installing the coil spring on a threaded sleeve attached to the shock

This SVT Focus was about to receive a serious suspension make over.

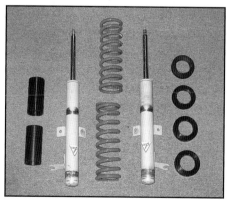

The Focus Central coil-over system was applied to the SVT Focus. The kit included Koni adjustable front struts along with an adjustable coil-over spring assembly.

The road race rear control arms featured provisions to mount a rear sway bar. Note the adjustments on the arms and the use of urethane end links.

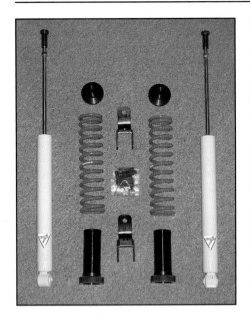

The rear kit included Koni adjustable shocks and Focus Central coil-over springs.

The first step was to remove the wheel. Note that this SVT had been previously equipped with H&R lowering springs and struts.

body. The Ground Control rear assembly added adjustability by installing a threaded upper spring perch, but did not incorporate the threaded section on the shock itself. This system was not a true coil-over assembly, but offered similar adjustability. Perhaps Ground Control was worried about concentrating all the spring load into the upper shock mount, an area never originally designed to take such loading.

Walter from Focus Central unbolted the lower strut retaining bolt, disconnected the brake hose and ABS wires from the strut housing, and unbolted the sway bar endlink.

The three upper strut retaining nuts were next on the list.

The stock (H&R) strut was removed and the spring separated from the strut using a spring compressor.

The upper bearing plate was utilized with the new Koni coil-over assembly.

Here is the completed assembly ready for installation onto the SVT Focus.

The new Koni assembly was pushed up into place and secured using the three upper mounting nuts. The stock hardware was reused.

Next came the rear sway bar end links. It was necessary to unbolt both sides before the rear suspension would move freely.

Walter then tightened the lower mounting bolt after properly positioning the strut.

The rear installation also began by removing the wheel and tire. Note that the rear suspension system differs from the front in that the shock and spring were separated.

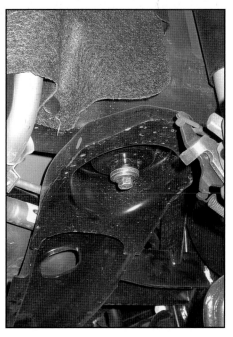

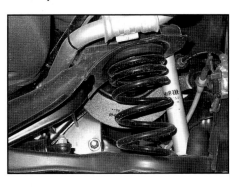

With a jack under the lower control arm, Walter unbolted the lower control arm mounting bolt and lowered the arm to remove the stock spring.

This shot better illustrates the locations of the rear shock and coil spring.

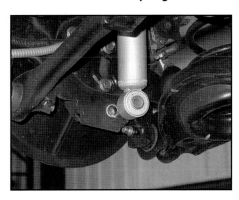

Here is the front coil-over assembly secured and in place.

Walter from Focus Central started by unbolting the lower shock mount.

It was necessary to unbolt the upper subframe mounting bolt.

This sub-frame mounting bolt was used to secure the upper (threaded) spring perch. It is this adjustable spring perch that allows adjustment of the ride height.

This kit differed slightly from the coil-over system installed on the ZX3 in that a separate (adjustable) spring was employed. This system retained the stock spring cup in the lower control arm.

The rear shock installation required removing a few interior panels.

Here is the completed rear SVT coil-over assembly installed and ready to go.

Building Better Binders: ZX3 Rear Disc Brake Upgrade

The standard Zetec Focus is a nimble vehicle, capable of acceptable levels of performance. The handling is above average, but the 2.0L Zetec motor is somewhat lacking in impressive performance. Curing the power problem was covered in the eight previous chapters, while further improving the handling was covered earlier in this chapter. Once you have more power and better handling, the next item on the to-do list would be brakes. Though adequate for the daily commute, the stock Zetec brakes become suspect when venturing out on the race track. The situation is compounded when adding a turbo or supercharger to the mix, as you are able to get up to speed that much quicker. All that go greatly increases the need for whoa. Unfortunately, the standard ZX3 is saddled with (of all things) rear drum brakes. I thought they stopped making those! Lucky for Focus enthusiasts, better binders are available right from your local Ford dealership. The system depicted here was put together by Focus Central, but all of the components were right from the parts shelf at your local Ford Dealer.

Here is what Ford should have put on the ZX3 Focus right from the start-rear disc brakes.

One of the complaints often lodged against he ZX3 Focus is the lack of adequate braking. Part of the reason for this can be attributed to the use of rear drum brakes.

The Focus Central rear disc brake upgrade kit featured all Ford factory parts.

The rear disc rotor measured 10 inches in diameter and featured slotting to improve cooling, reduce buildup of pad dust, and allow out-gassing.

The calipers were single-piston units.

The brake upgrade kit also included a new spindle and hub/bearing assembly.

Why should the SVT owners get all the stopping power?

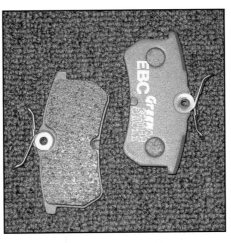

The kit included EBC Green Stuff brake pads for maximum braking performance.

Here is the rear kit installed on a ZX3 Focus. Note the factory appearance-not surprising since all factory parts were used.

Focus Central also sells an upgrade for the factory front brakes.

In an effort to reduce weight and improve cooling, Focus Central treated these factory rotors to extensive cross drilling. Stay away from this extreme measure for street use.

For their race car, Focus Central opted for a set of ultra-light Wilwood front brakes. The Wilwoods reduced unsprung weight by as much as 30 pounds per side.

Getting Hooked Up: Clutch, Flywheel, and Limited-Slip Diff Install

The transmission upgrades depicted here came out of necessity. While experimenting with the prototype M62 Jackson Racing supercharger kit (see chapter 8 for details on the engine buildup), the additional power supplied by the supercharger and other mods play havoc on the stock clutch. In defense of the stock unit, Ford obviously never envisioned the Zetec motor producing more than double its original output. While the stock clutch seemed to hold up fine on

Jimmy Privett of Aasco Motorsports separated the case to allow access to the factory (open) differential.

out just how much clamping pressure is required for the power output of the motor. Actually, a number of other variables will affect clutch strength (or lack thereof), including vehicle weight, available traction (slicks, fwd, 4wd etc…) and even driver attitude. If you are the kind of person that leaves every stop light in a flurry of tire smoke, chances are that your clutch won't last nearly as long as a more sane individual. Ditto for those enthusiasts who constantly ride the clutch, effectively burning the linings out of them. The strength (or ability to handle torque) of a clutch is determined by a number of variables as well, including clamping pressure from the pressure plate, changes in the surface area (size) of the friction material, and changes in the friction material itself. Obviously the clamping pressure produced by the pressure plate affects the holding power of the clutch. More pressure applied by the pressure plate to the clutch disc equals more holding power, but not without a trade-off. Excessive pressure creates

the dyno, attempting to post quick e.t.s at the local drag strip resulted in nothing but slippage and the attending frustration. There is nothing worse than having the power to vanquish your competitor only to watch them motor off into the sunset while you nurse a slipping clutch through the traps. On the one hand it was good that the supercharged Zetec motor was producing so much additional power, but not being able to put it to the pavement was starting to take its toll. In the end, it was time to yank the tranny and install a new clutch. While the tranny was out, we decided to install a couple of other mods that would ultimately help acceleration.

The adventure began when I decided

Focus Central supplied this 4.30 Gear set for the MTX75 tranaxle.

that it should be possible for a ZX3 Focus to out-accelerate a stock Mustang GT. Equipped with a 4.6L V8 (circa 2001), the modular Mustang GT motors pumped out 260 flywheel horsepower. Though double the power output of the standard 2.0L Zetec motor, the Focus was considerably lighter than the big Mustang. The reasoning went that it should be possible to achieve equal or better acceleration using equal power and a lighter vehicle, all we had to do was get the Zetec motor to produce 260 flywheel horsepower (roughly 235 wheel hp). We knew going in that doubling the power output of the Zetec motor would be difficult but not impossible using forced induction. We also knew that even equipped with a supercharger, the Zetec motor would never equal the torque production (or therefore average power production) of the bigger V8, but we hoped that the lower curb weight would offset that advantage.

After installing a number of mods including the M62 supercharger kit from Jackson Racing, we eventually reached the power goal, with the Zetec pumping out 237 wheel horsepower. Now all we had to do was get it hooked up.

One of the problems with choosing a clutch for a given application is figuring

The factory diff was in plain view and easily removed after initial case separation.

Ford Racing supplied a T-2 Torsen (Torque Sensing) limited slip differential for this ZX3 tranny. The Torsen T-2 is shown next to the stock open differential.

problems with pedal effort and throwout bearing life, neither of which is desirable. There is nothing worse that sitting in bumper-to-bumper traffic with a pressure plate that requires a double leg press to engage.

One of the more effective routes, and one less likely to result in leg cramps, is to alter the friction material, or more specifically the amount of material in contact with the flywheel and pressure plate. The clutch disc acts as the intermediary between the engine and transmission. Splined to the input shaft of the transmission (or transaxle), the clutch transmits the power from the engine to the transmission. To do this, it must be engaged (held by pressure) against the flywheel while engaged (via splines) to the tranny—no easy task. Though transmitting power once the clutch disc is engaged is not difficult, it is the engagement process that creates problems. Think about what happens when you dump the clutch even at a realistic engine speed of just 2,500 rpm. The spinning flywheel (with plenty of inertia) meets the stationary clutch disc. The motor wants to spin but the clutch (and attached tranny, diff and tires) all want to stop the engine. Of course the power of the engine overcomes the stalling process and we achieve acceleration. Along the way, the clutch is subjected to slippage, as the stalled drive train and the spinning motor achieve equilibrium. It is this slippage that not only creates clutch wear but also taxes the ability of the clutch to transmit the power effectively.

One method of improving the ability of the clutch to withstand this abuse is to alter the amount of material in contact with either the flywheel or pressure plate. Oddly enough, to increase the clamp load (measured in pounds per square inch) you actually reduce the surface area of the friction material. Lets say we have a pressure plate supplying 100 pounds per square inch over a clutch disc surface area of 39 square inches.

If we decrease the surface area of the clutch by replacing the conventional (organic) disc with a racy 6-puck style (like the one we used on the Project Focus), the point loading on the friction material actually increases. Simple math tell us that if you keep the load constant (by retaining the same pressure plate) while reducing the surface area (swapping clutch discs), you increase the pounds per square inch on the individual pucks. Stick with me here, as it gets more interesting. Though the point loading has increased, you have decreased the surface area, resulting in a wash in overall available friction. The key to increased clutch performance (friction) is to alter the friction material itself. A change in friction material will certainly make a noticeable change in the clutch performance. In the case of our fast Focus, the Aasco test fixture indicated that our stock clutch and pressure plate required 230 pounds of breakaway torque. The disc upgrade provided by Clutch Net (to a 6-puck sintered Bronze material) increased the breakaway torque figure to 320 pounds—an increase in clamping power of 43%.

Sealer was applied to the outer edge of the tranny casing.

All that was left after installing the tranny case was to hook up the shifter and other minor accessories.

While everything was disassembled, we decided to upgrade to an aluminum flywheel as well. The aluminum flywheel was supplied by Aasco Performance. Flywheels are tricky business, especially when the flywheel incorporates tricky bits like a crank position sensor along with the usual ring gear for starter engagement. The major benefit of the Aasco aluminum flywheel was obvious weight savings. The stock iron Zetec flywheel weighed in at a hefty 22.5 pounds. Adding the stock 3-pound disc and 9.5-pound pressure plate resulted in a total rotating weight of 35 pounds. Replacing the stock flywheel with the lighter Aasco piece resulted in a reduction of 11 pounds from the total weight. The aluminum flywheel was just over 1/2 the weight of the cast iron stocker. Though any weight loss equals more performance (an increase in power-to-weight ratio equals improved acceleration), reciprocating weight is doubly important. The motor must work to accelerate this mass, and less mass is easier to accelerate. The motor was much

The new ring gear supplied by Focus Central was installed onto the T-2 Torsen differential.

The new ring gear and diff assembly were reinstalled. Note the new differential bearing.

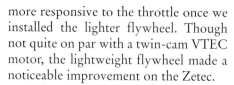

While we had the tranny out, we decided to upgrade from the stock steel flywheel to a lightweight unit from Aasco Motorsports.

The Aasco flywheel featured a pinned ring gear. These dowels were used to secure the ring gear in place.

Naturally a clutch upgrade was necessary, as the stock clutch was no match for the power produced by the supercharged motor. Power Tone supplied the disc and pressure plate for the supercharged Zetec. Both clamping force and disc material were upgraded on the new clutch.

more responsive to the throttle once we installed the lighter flywheel. Though not quite on par with a twin-cam VTEC motor, the lightweight flywheel made a noticeable improvement on the Zetec.

When installing an aluminum flywheel there is one critical element, namely the friction surface. Obviously aluminum (even the 6061-T6 used on the flywheel) is considerably softer than cast iron. The clutch disc usually contacts a surface machined into the cast iron flywheel. If we tried this on aluminum, the results would be less than spectacular. The soft(er) aluminum would wear rather quickly and soon enough the disc would eat itself all the way through the fancy aluminum flywheel. To stop this from happening, a steel friction surface is bolted to the aluminum flywheel. Obviously the steel insert increases the weight of the assembly, but it is weight well spent considering the alternative. The critical element in the steel friction surface is the thickness. Install a friction sur-

face that is too thin may result in warpage once friction heat is applied. The aluminum Zetec Focus flywheel supplied by Aasco featured a beefy 3/8-inch thick friction surface to eliminate any chance of warping. The Aasco aluminum flywheel also featured a pinned starter ring gear. Though pressed on (after heating the gear), Aasco drilled holes intersecting the steel ring gear and aluminum outer diameter and then inserted steel pins to lock the gear in place. It is precision machining and taking the extra steps like pinning the ring gear that make for a quality product.

While the tranny was out, we also took the opportunity to install a limited slip differential from the X-treme Performance lineup in the Ford Racing catalog. Like the offerings for the Mustang guys, the Ford Racing catalog is full of performance goodies for us cylinder-challenged Focus owners as well. With everything from superchargers (like our Jackson Racing unit) to complete engine

assemblies, we were happy (though not surprised) to find the Torsen T-2 traction differential offered by Ford Racing. If nothing else, we can brag to our fellow Focus owners that we have the very same diff used in the 304 horsepower (turbocharged) Ford Racing FR200 Focus. Unlike either conventional clutch-type or even speed-sensing limited-slip differentials, the Torsen was a full-time, torque-sensing, torque-biasing differential. This combination allowed immediate response to variable driving conditions according to Ford Racing. What this meant for our supercharged Focus was added traction when hitting the line under boost. Traction was obviously limited with our one-legged factory differential. By no means a powerhouse, even a stock Focus can spin the tires if provoked. The Torsen diff would help give us an edge when pulling up to the line against our nemesis, the 4.6L Mustang. Jimmy Privett from Aasco Motorsports made short work of installing the T-2 diff (and Focus Central gear set) into our MTX-75 transaxle.

Author's Note – Thanks goes out to the gang at Jackson Racing for all their help with the supercharged project. Not only did they help with the tranny R&R, but Oscar himself even jumped in and performed most of the labor. Jimmy Privett over at Aasco Motorsports installed the performance components into the Focus tranny. Without the help of these guys, the supercharged Focus would never have dipped into the 13s.

The tranny upgrades helped get the supercharged ZX3 into the 13s way back in 2001. Here is the author at the line ready to rip off a high 13 and put a hurting on the fellow in the next lane.

FOCUS PERFORMANCE SOURCE GUIDE

Aasco Performance
(714) 758-8500
www.aascoperformance.com

Advanced Clutch Technology
P.O. Box 903425
Palmdale, CA 93590
(661) 947-7791

AEM
2205 126th St. Unit A
Hawthorne, CA 90250
(310) 484-2322
www.aempower.com

Arias
13420 S. Normandie Ave.
Gardina, CA 90249
(310) 532-9737
www.ariaspistons.com

ARP
531 Spectrum Circle
Oxnard, CA 93030
(805) 278-7223

Baer Racing
3108 West Thomas Rd St1201
Phoenix, AZ 85017
(602) 233-1411
www.baer.com

Best Products/ProM
21890 Meyers Rd.
Oak Park, MI 48237
(248) 399-9223

Borla Performance Industries
5901 Edison Dr.
Oxnard, CA 93033
877-Go Borla
www.Borla.com

Coast High Performance/Probe
1650 W. 228th St.
Torrance, CA 90501
(310) 784-2977
www.347streetfighter.com

Comp Cams/ZEX
3406 Democratt Rd.
Memphis, TN 38118
(901) 795-2400

Crane Cams
530 Fentress Blvd.
Daytona Beach, FL 32114
(904) 252-1151
www.cranecams.com

Crower Cams & Equipment
3333 Main St.
Chula Vista, CA 91911
(619) 422-1191

Denso
3900 Via Oro Ave
Long Beach, CA 90810
(888) 511-4312
www.densoiridium.com

Eagle
8530 Aaron Lane
Southhaven, MS 38671
(662) 796-7373

Extrude Hone
Ed Meledez
8800 Somerset Blvd
Paramount, CA 90723
(562) 531-2976

Fel Pro
One Equation Blvd.
Ashland, MS 38603
(662) 224-8972
www.federal-mogul.com

F-Max
1175 Industrial Ave. Unit R
Escondido, CA 92029
(760) 746-6638
www.f-max.com

Focus Central
426 North Curry
Tehachapi, CA 93561
(661) 823-2400
www.focuscentral.com

Ford Racing Performance Parts
P.O. Box 51394
Livonia, MI 48151
(586) 468-1356

Gude Performance
29885 2nd St Unit Q
Lake Elsinore, CA 92530
(909) 244-3533
www.gude.com

Holley/Hooker
1801 Russellville Rd.
PO Box 10360
Bowling Green, KY 42102
1 (800) Holley 1

Innovative Turbo Systems
845 Easy Street, Unit 102
Simi Valley, CA 93065
(805) 526-5400
www.innovativeturbo.com

Jacobs Electronics
500 N Baird St.
Midland, TX 79701
(915) 685-3345
www.jacobs.com

Jackson Racing
440 Rutherford St.
Goletta, CA 93117
(888) 888-4079
www.jacksonracing.com

JBA
7149 Mission Gorge Rd
San Diego, CA 92120
(619) 229-7797

JE Pistons
15312 Connector Ln
Huntington Beach, CA 92649
(714) 373-5530

K&N Engineering
P.O. Box 1329
1455 Citrus Ave.
Riverside, CA 92502
(909) 826-4000
www.knfilters.com

Kenne Bell
10743 Bell Ct.
Rancho Cucamonga, CA 91730
(909) 941-6646

Killer Bee Racing
15561 Product Ln. Suite D1
Huntington Beach, CA 92649
(714) 901-9101

Moroso Performance Products
80 Carter Dr.
PO Box 1470
Guilford, CT 06437
(203) 453-6571
www.moroso.com

MSD
1490 Henry Brennan Dr.
El Paso, Texas 79936
(915) 857-3344

Pectel Technologies
25 Spectrum Point Drive, Suite 401
Lake Forest, CA 92630
(949) 586-3609
www.pectelusa.com

PowerTrain Dynamics
15628 Graham St.
Huntington Beach, CA 92649
(714) 373-0068

RC Engineering
1728 Border Ave.
Torrance, CA 90501
(310) 320-2277
www.rceng.com

Redline Oil
(800) 624-7958
www.redlineoil.com

Sho Shop
15608 Graham St.
Huntington Beach, CA 92649
(714) 894-8415

Steeda
(954) 960-0774
www.steeda.com

TurboXS
267 Kentlands Blvd #3043
Gaithersburg, MD 20878
(877) 887-2679

Turbonetics/Spearco
2255 Agate Ct.
Simi Valley, CA 93065
(805) 581-0333
www.turboneticsinc.com

Turbo City
1137 West Katella Ave.
Orange, CA 92867
(714) 639-4933
www.turbocity.com

Unorthodox Racing
11 Brandywine Dr.
Dearpark, NY 11729
(631) 253-4909
www.info@unorthodoxracing.com

Vortech
1650 Pacific Ave
Channel Islands, CA 93033
(805) 247-0226